Geotext

1

PEARSON
Longman

Clare Brooks Karen Holdich Garrett Nagle Jo Norcup
Series Editor: Olly Phillipson

Contents

1·1 What's it all about?

Geography is a journey in time and space that we make every day. As a school subject, geography is concerned with the study of the world – its people and places. The word geography means 'Earth-writing'.

Geographers study the world. They look at the links between people and their **environments**. They highlight **patterns** and **processes** and try to explain them. They try to predict what changes might take place and consider different viewpoints or **philosophies**. Being a geographer means experiencing the world, but also understanding your local environment.

Geography takes place all the time in our daily lives. We try to make sense of the world from what we see, hear, feel and experience – by reading, listening, watching and doing. Geography is a subject about **interactions** that happen all around us, changing over time.

> What do you know about the world around you – its people and environments? Where have you learned about the world from?

▼ Figure 1: How geography links with other subjects

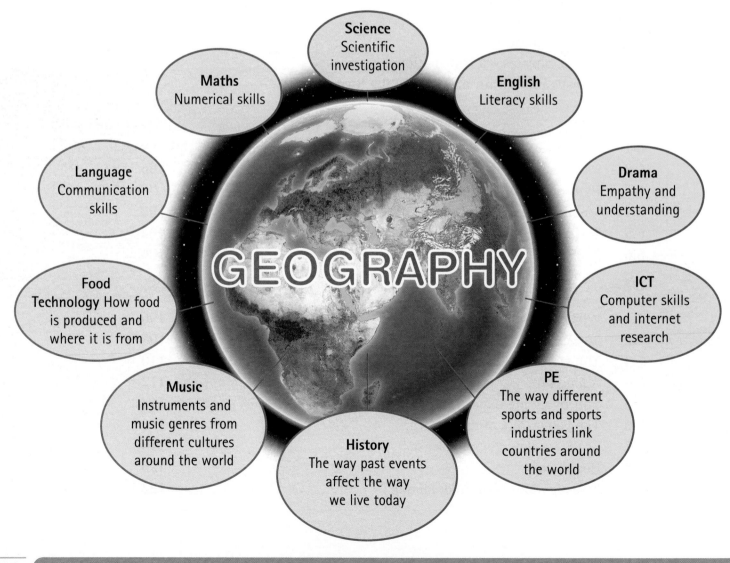

Key Words: philosophies see page 124

Geographers as detectives

Geographers need to have a wide range of skills to:

- produce, use and analyse data
- undertake fieldwork and surveys
- draw detailed diagrams and sketches
- use a wide range of resource material.

Geographers use these skills like detectives to try to understand our world, planet Earth. But why?

The Earth keeps us alive by giving us the air we breathe, places to live, and feeding and clothing us. Just by living we (and other living things) have an impact on the world. If we don't understand how we impact on the Earth and how it impacts on us, then we might cause permanent damage. Geography isn't just about finding out about different places, it's about finding out how and why we live like we do, and how we can make the world better for ourselves and others.

Look carefully at the photographs in Figures 2 and 3. Think about *where* they might have been taken. What clues are there in the photos that help tell you about the location? What is happening here? Who might have taken the photos? Why was it taken?

> Write down your own questions about the photographs and see what you can find out about them.

▼ Figure 2: City shopping – where?

▼ Figure 3: Night time – where?

The big questions

Geographers need a wide range of skills and abilities to investigate the 'big questions'. To be a geographer means asking lots of questions about the world and trying to figure out why things happen. It also involves thinking about what this could mean for the future.

Geographers need to ask

Why? What? When? How? Who?

Over time, geographers have developed different ways and ideas to investigate the world. **Socrates** was one of the first modern **philosophers** and one of the first geographers. He had a great influence on the way that geographers developed an understanding of the world. He did not accept what society told him the world was like, but constantly observed and investigated it himself, continually asking 'big questions' to help understand it.

▼ Figure 1: People who have influenced geographical enquiry

▼ Albert Einstein

(died 1955): a scientist who described himself as being 'passionately curious'

▼ Charles Darwin

(died 1882): made connections between animals, environments and the theory of evolution

▼ Galileo

(died 1642): discovered that the Earth is round and orbits the sun

▼ Francis Drake

(died 1596): an English explorer who sailed around the world in the sixteenth century

◀ Socrates (died 399 BC): one of the world's first geographers

Think of five 'big questions' *you* have about the world. For example: Why do we have oceans and seas on the Earth? What do they do?

Many philosophers from Ancient Rome and Greece discussed their theories about the world by setting hypotheses. A **hypothesis** is a theory that can be investigated and tested in different ways. For example, a hypothesis could be thinking that local places are easier to understand than those further away. Testing and proving hypotheses have been important in the development of subjects like science, maths and geography.

Between the fifteenth and sixteenth centuries, European geographers and explorers travelled across the world. They had to find different methods to understand the many new places and people they came across.

Explorers, such as Marco Polo, Francis Drake and James Cook, sailed around the world in search of new lands. Biologists, including Alfred Wallace and Charles Darwin, travelled the world to find, observe and map different types of plants and wildlife.

Scientists, mathematicians and astronomers developed new techniques to measure and monitor the world. This allowed humans to understand the way the world worked. It helped them to see patterns or suggest grand theories to help them. Galileo's scientific research confirmed that the Earth was round and that it travelled around the Sun – something that people previously didn't think happened!

Geography is a combination of past histories and theories, plus more recent views on the world as it is today. All of this, past *and* present, is open to discussion, debate and change.

Figure 2: Answering the 'big questions'

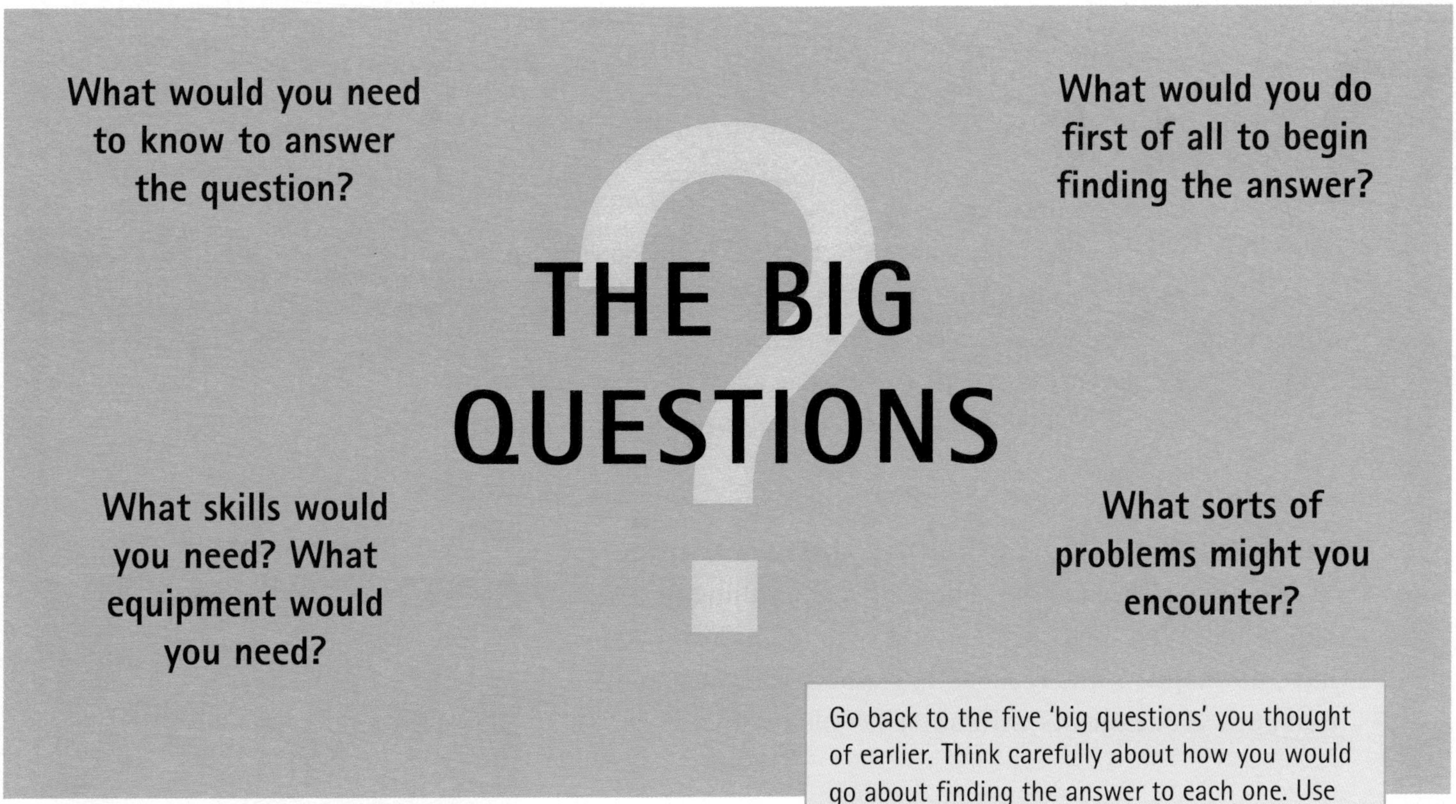

What would you need to know to answer the question?

What would you do first of all to begin finding the answer?

THE BIG QUESTIONS

What skills would you need? What equipment would you need?

What sorts of problems might you encounter?

Go back to the five 'big questions' you thought of earlier. Think carefully about how you would go about finding the answer to each one. Use **Figure 2** to help you.

Key Words: hypothesis see page 124

1·3 Using geography

You are already a geographer

Geographers try to understand how events can affect people and places. Let's take an example and see what you already know...

Yesterday it was announced that the Local Education Authority wants to close your school. Once you have stopped celebrating (!), think about how this might affect you, and your local community. Consider where you would have to go to school.

You and your family:
- How might this change your journey to school?
- How might this affect what you do before and after school?
- How might it affect your family?
- Decide if this is a positive or a negative change, and give one reason why.

Your teachers and other school staff:
- How might this change affect your teachers?
- Do your teachers live in the local area?
- Are there other schools nearby with job vacancies? How might they travel there?
- How might it affect staff working part-time or with families to take care of?
- Decide if this is a positive or a negative change, and give one reason why.

Local community
- How might this change affect the shops around your school?
- How might it affect local bus routes?
- What would happen to the school site?
- How might changes in the future affect the local area?
- Decide if this is a positive or a negative change, and give one reason why.

Look back at the decisions you've made

Overall, would closing the school be a good thing or a bad thing? Who might benefit and who might lose? You have developed some reasons to support your argument. Compare your reasons with other people in your class.

▼ Figure 1: A derelict school

Planning and building a school

Okay, they are not really closing your school. But if they did, what would you want your new school to be like?

Schools are generally built to serve the local community, so it would need to be close to where people live. You would need suitable land for buildings and some open space for break-times and sport. Transport links are important but can be added after the school has been built. Consider also if the school building should be made available to other community members outside of school hours.

Part 1

- What questions would you ask before building a new school? Here are some to start you thinking – you need to add more of your own and make a list …
  - Where would the school be built?
  - Who would use the school?
  - What would the building be made of?
  - What transport would be used to get students and teachers to and from school?
  - How would the school be powered?
  - Would you have classrooms?
  - What technology would you need?

Part 2

- On a map of your local area, try to find a suitable space for your new school.
- Do you think the local people would agree with your decision about where to locate it?
- Prepare a short, illustrated presentation of your ideas about a new school.

Debrief

You have been able to do this activity by using your own geographical knowledge about your local area. There will be a range of views about this local issue, but most of them are connected to geography.
Well done!

▼ Figure 2: A new school

2·1 Maps past and present

A map is a picture that shows information about a place. Different maps show what the map maker wants them to. They may highlight particular features rather than others. This means that maps can be used as political tools to deliver certain messages. If you look at atlases produced in different countries, the world map will usually show the home country and continent in the centre. For example, most world maps shown here have the UK and Europe in the centre.

The history of maps

The Mappa Mundi [Figure 1] is a thirteenth-century map of the world. It shows Asia at the top of the map, and Africa and Europe below. (The Americas had not yet been discovered by Europeans.) Jerusalem is in the centre, reflecting religious belief rather than geographic fact. Accurate large scale world maps date from the 1580s. Before that many maps were more like pictures, often drawn from imaginative descriptions of travellers' tales.

▼ Figure 1: An extract from the Mappa Mundi

▼ Figure 2: The Mercator projection

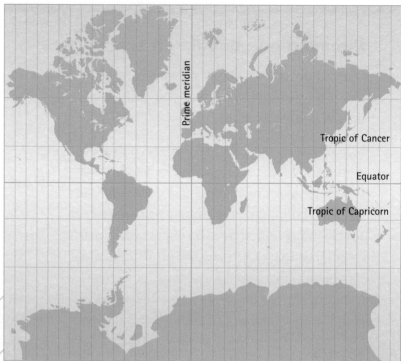

The Mercator projection in a UK atlas puts Europe in the centre

Using projections

World maps show location by lines of **latitude** (how far north or south of the Equator a place is) and lines of **longitude** (how far east or west of the Prime Meridian, Greenwich, a place is). Dimension presents a difficulty when mapping the world. The most accurate way is to create a three-dimensional globe, but it is easier to use a two-dimensional map. However, the surface of the Earth is curved – and a map is flat. Our maps therefore have to show reality in different ways by using different **projections.**

The most commonly used world map is the Mercator projection [Figure 2]. It is centred on Europe, and emphasises areas away from the Equator. The shapes of the continents are accurate, but not their sizes.

Key Words: latitude, longitude, projections see page 124

Figure 3: Gall's projection ▶

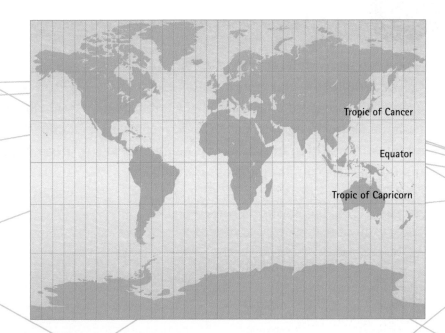

Tropic of Cancer

Equator

Tropic of Capricorn

Another version is Gall's projection [Figure 3]. This slightly distorts both size and shape. As a result, temperate regions (areas separating the pole from the tropics) appear to take up a larger area than in the Mercator projection.

▼ Figure 4: The Peters' projection

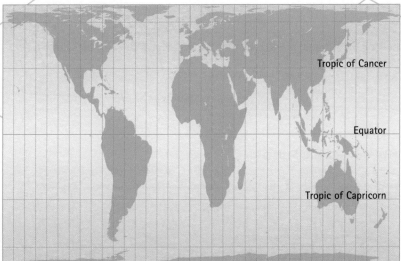

Tropic of Cancer

Equator

Tropic of Capricorn

One of the most recent map projections is the Peters' map [Figure 4]. It was first published in the 1970s and caused much debate because it looked so different to other projections. It is an 'Equal Area' projection giving countries their correct size but distorting their shape. It emphasises the size of poorer LEDCs compared to richer MEDCs.

▼ Figure 5: The Oblique Aitoff projection

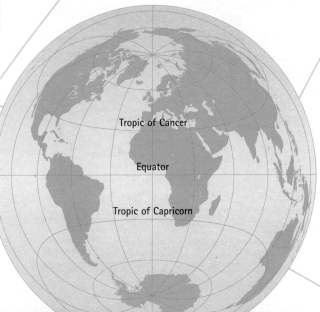

Tropic of Cancer

Equator

Tropic of Capricorn

The Aitoff projection [Figure 5] is, like Peters, an Equal Area map. It is useful for focusing on a hemisphere, continent or polar region – for example, to show aircraft routes. However, it becomes increasingly distorted at the edges.

Make up a table showing different map projections, how they show the world, and their different uses. Find out about other map projections not mentioned here.

2·2 Types of maps

There are many different types of maps. In the UK, geographers – and others – often use maps produced by the Ordnance Survey (OS), the UK's national mapping agency. Each OS map contains a huge amount of information and being able to read them is an important geographical skill.

OS maps are produced at many different scales [Figure 1]. Each scale has its own set of symbols and range of uses. Larger scale maps show less detail than smaller scale maps, but cover bigger areas [Figures 2 and 3]. The 1:25 000 (Explorer) and 1:50 000 (Landranger) OS maps are the most widely used.

▼ Figure 1: OS maps of different scales

Name of map	Scale	What is shown
Route	1:625 000	All of the UK on one double-sided map.
Road	1:250 000	Eight regional maps cover the country.
Landranger	1:50 000	204 Landranger maps cover the country. Each map covers an area of 40 km by 40 km.
Explorer	1:25 000	403 maps cover every part of England, Scotland and Wales. Each map covers an area of 30 km by 20 km.
Landplan	1:10 000	Very detailed, showing individual houses. Each map covers an area of 5 km by 5 km.
Superplan	1:1 250 (urban) 1:2 500 (rural)	The most detailed maps available. Each map covers an area of only 400m by 400m (urban) or 800m by 800m (rural)

▼ Figure 2: 1:625 000 Route map

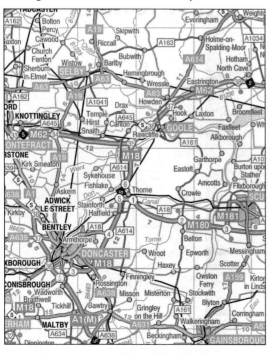

▼ Figure 3: 1:2 000 Superplan

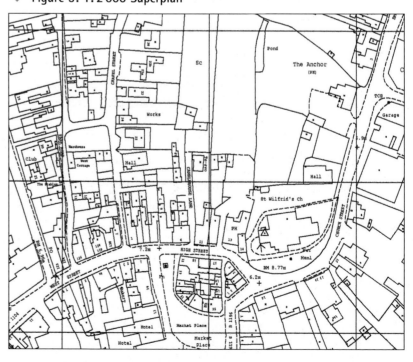

Figure 4: London Underground map

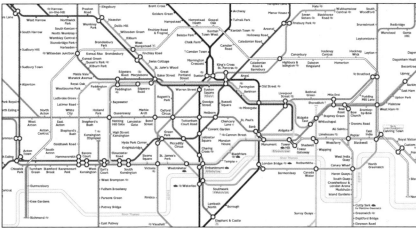

Apart from OS maps, the variety and range of maps we use is huge. **Figure 4** is a **topological map** showing part of the London Underground system. It distorts real distances and shapes to show a simpler, clearer image that is easier to use and understand.

Other maps are for more specialist use. These include **synoptic weather maps** [Figure 5] which show actual and forecast weather. Geological maps show the type of rock found underground beneath the soil. This is important information for a range of people including farmers, builders, water companies and gardeners.

Some maps show imaginary places. JRR Tolkein's map of Middle Earth from his Lord of the Rings trilogy and Robert Louis Stevenson's map of Treasure Island [**Figure 6**] are two of the most well known.

Figure 5: Synoptic weather map

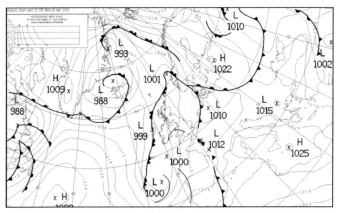

Figure 6: Map of Robert Louis Stevenson's Treasure Island

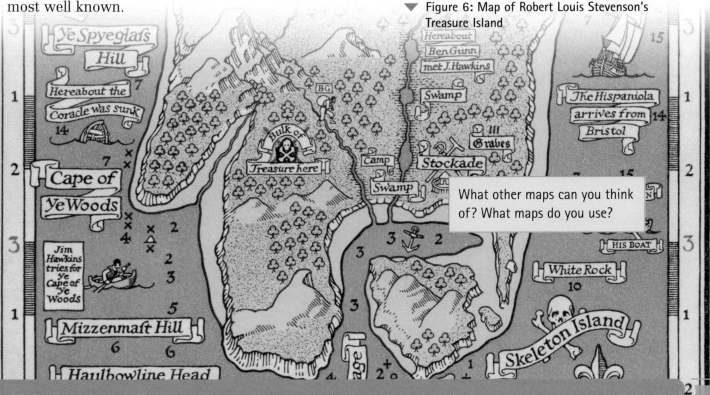

What other maps can you think of? What maps do you use?

OS map literacy 1

Scale, distance and direction

Being able to read a book means that you are **literate** – but good geographers have to be map literate as well. Just like books, maps need to be read, but as well as using words they show information using symbols, numbers and colours.

Scale and distance

Scale is a way of reducing the size of a geographical area so that it can fit onto a map. Scale can be shown on maps in several ways – as a statement, a **ratio**, a fraction or as a **linear scale**.

One way of working out distance on a map is to use the ratio. As the number on the right-hand side of the ratio gets smaller, the area covered by the map also gets smaller. The smaller the area is, the greater the detail that can be shown.

Figure 1 shows how to work out distances on a map using a ratio.

Think up a good way to remember the relationship between different scales and what maps show.

▼ Figure 1: How to work out distances from a ratio

1: 50 000	1: 25 000
1 cm on the map equals 50 000 cm or 0.5 km on the ground	1 cm on the map equals 25 000 cm or 0.25 km on the ground
This means that 2 cm on the map equals 1 km on the ground	This means that 4 cm on the map equals 1 km on the ground
Any distance in cm must be divided by 2 to give the distance in km, e.g. 4.8 cm on the map equals 2.4 km on the ground	Any distance in cm must be divided by 4 to give the distance in km, e.g. 4.8 cm on the map equals 1.2 km on the ground

Another way of working out distance on an OS map is by using a linear scale [Figure 2]. Measure the distance between two places with a ruler. Place the ruler along the linear scale and you will be able to see the distance in kilometres.

▼ Figure 2: Using a linear scale on a 1: 50 000 scale map

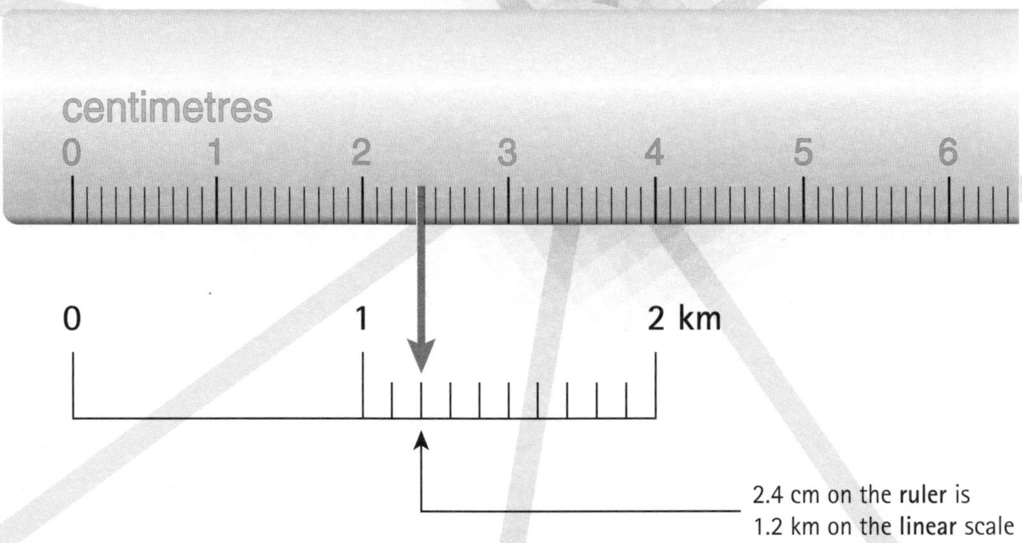

centimetres
0   1   2   3   4   5   6

0   1   2 km

2.4 cm on the **ruler** is
1.2 km on the **linear** scale

To measure curved distances, for example a river:

- lay a piece of string along what you want to measure
- use a ruler or the linear scale on the map to measure the length of the string
- work out the actual length or distance in kilometres.

If you prefer, use the edge of a piece of paper:

- place the piece of paper on the curved route you want to measure
- mark off straight line sections on the paper with a pencil
- move the paper to the next section, starting from your last pencil mark and continue marking sections until you have finished
- use a ruler or the linear scale on the map to measure the length from the first to the last pencil mark
- work out the actual length or distance in kilometres.

Direction

Direction is measured using a compass. The four main points of the compass are shown in **red** in [Figure 4]. You can remember their order with a **mnemonic** starting at the top and going clockwise: **N**aughty **E**lephants **S**quirt **W**ater. It is also useful to know the four secondary points of the compass, as shown in **blue**.

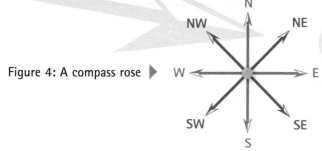

Figure 4: A compass rose ▶

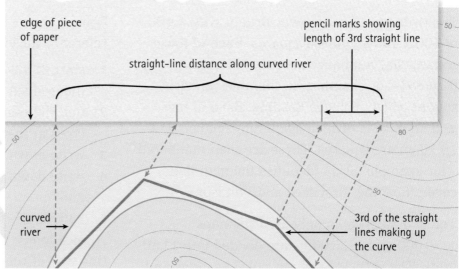

▼ Figure 3: Measuring curved distances (e.g. a river) on maps

edge of piece of paper

pencil marks showing length of 3rd straight line

straight-line distance along curved river

curved river →

3rd of the straight lines making up the curve

Every map should have a north arrow. Unless the north arrow tells you otherwise, north is always at the top of a map.

Make up your own mnemonic to help remember compass directions.

▼ Figure 5: How to work out a compass direction

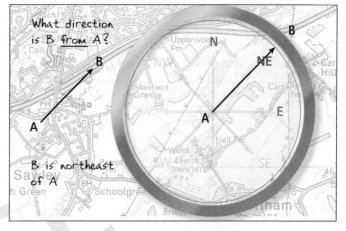

To work out the direction *from* place A to place B, imagine place A is in the centre of the compass rose. Follow one of the arms in the direction of B [Figure 5].

2·4 OS map literacy 2

Grid references

The Ordnance Survey cover Britain with a grid of 100 x 100 kilometre squares. Each of these squares has a unique two-letter identity [Figure 1]. For example, SU identifies the grid square which includes Reading. Each of these grid squares is divided again into smaller 10 x 10 kilometre squares. These are then numbered – for example, SU65 identifies the map that covers Reading, Bracknell and Windsor.

The two most commonly used OS maps – 1 : 50 000 and 1 : 25 000 – are divided into 1 km² grids. The vertical lines are called eastings and the horizontal lines are called northings. Each line has a two-figure number. We can use these numbers to give four or six-figure grid references to locate any place or feature on the map.

▼ Figure 1: OS grid squares

HL	HM	HN	HO	HP	JL	JM
HQ	HR	HS	HT	HU	JQ	JR
HV	HW	HX	HY	HZ	JV	JW
NA	NB	NC	ND	NE	OA	OB
NF	NG	NH	NJ	NK	OF	OG
NL	NM	NN	NO	NP	OL	OM
NQ	NR	NS	NT	NU	OQ	OR
NV	NW	NX	NY	NZ	OV	OW
SA	SB	SC	SD	SE	TA	TB
SF	SG	SH	SJ	SK	TF	TG
SL	SM	SN	SO	SP	TL	TM
SQ	SR	SS	ST	SU	TQ	TR
SV	SW	SX	SY	SZ	TV	TW

Four-figure grid references

Figure 2 shows how to work out a four-figure grid reference for location Z:

1. start in the bottom left (southwest) corner of the grid square
2. find the numbers of the two gridlines that cross at that point
3. write down the easting number first = 23
4. write down the northing number after it = 2357
5. 2357 is the four-figure grid reference for location Z.

One way of remembering this is that you must walk along a corridor before you can climb the stairs. Grid references are written differently from co-ordinates in mathematics. There is no space or comma between them and they have brackets around them.

▼ Figure 2: Four–figure grid references

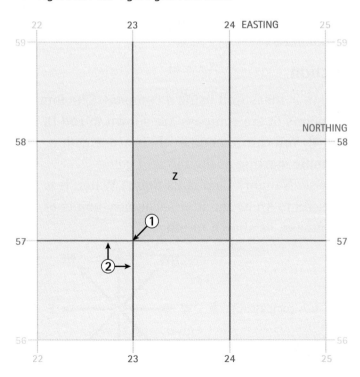

Six-figure grid references

A more accurate location can be given by using six-figure grid references. **Figure 3** shows how to work out a six-figure grid reference. To work out the six-figure grid reference for location Z:

1 start in the bottom left (south-west) corner of the grid square

2 imagine that each grid square is divided into a grid of 10 x 10 smaller squares

3 work out the easting by estimating how many small grid squares or tenths you must move to the right (east)

4 the easting for Z is 4 tenths right (east) of gridline 23, so it will be 234

5 work out the northing by estimating how many small grid squares or tenths you must move upwards (north)

6 the northing for Z is 6 tenths up (north) of gridline 57, so it will be 576

7 this means that the six-figure grid reference for Z is 234576.

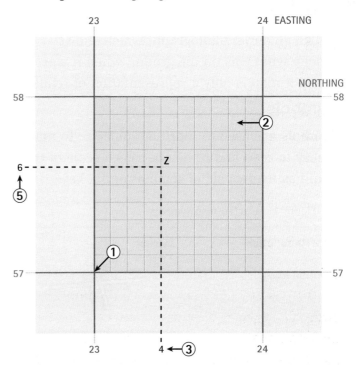

▼ Figure 3: Six-figure grid references

Think of a good, but simple, way to remember which way round to give grid references.

Look at the small 1:50 000 map extract [**Figure 4**]. Use it to practice looking up and giving grid references. Make up a set of five questions for each of the following:

1 Give the four-figure grid reference for a square with named features in it.

2 Give the six-figure grid reference for a named place or feature.

3 Look up the following grid squares. Name two or three main features in each one.

4 Look up the following six-figure grid references. What is found in each location?

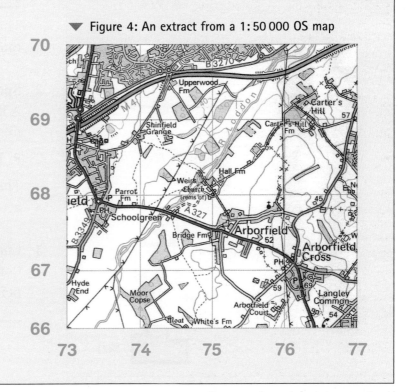

▼ Figure 4: An extract from a 1:50 000 OS map

2·5 OS map literacy 3

Unlike an aerial photograph, which shows exactly what was on the ground when it was taken, a map is only a representation of reality.

Symbols

Symbols are used to represent objects. To make it easy to read and remember, each scale of OS map has its own set of symbols and a key.

▼ Figure 1: Selected map symbols

Description	Symbol
buildings	
motorway	M1
main road	A414
secondary road	B1072
railway line	
railway station	
non-coniferous woodland	
National Trust area	
viewpoint	
school	Sch

Figure 1 shows some of the symbols used on a 1:50 000 scale map.

> What do you think of the symbols in **Figure 1**? Make up you own alternatives. They should be easy to use and remember.

Relief

Relief means the height and shape of the land.

A map is a two-dimensional representation of the three-dimensional world, so map makers need to find ways of showing height. Three main ways are used on an OS map:

1 **Triangulation pillars**
   Also called trig points. A blue triangle with a number to indicate the number of metres above sea level.

    246

   They are found at the top of hills and mountains.

2 **Spot heights**
   A black dot with a number to indicate the number of metres above sea level.

   • 14

   They are found along roads in relatively flat areas.

3 **Contours**
   Contours are brown lines which join together points of the same height above sea level.

—— 40 ——

Contours

Contours are drawn at intervals of 10 metres on a 1:50 000 map and 5 metres on a 1:25 000 map. At every 50 metres on a 1:50 000 map and every 25 metres on a 1:25 000 map the contour is drawn as a thicker line.

Not every contour has its height above sea level written on it, but it is possible to work out its height from other contours or nearby information on the map. For example, if a contour is drawn between the 30- and 50-metre contours it will be 40 metres above sea level.

If contours are close together they indicate a steep slope. Very steep or vertical slopes or cliffs have their own symbol.

If contours are far apart they indicate a gentle slope. **Figure 2** shows how to identify slopes and common landforms from the shape of contour lines. Learning to recognise these shapes will help you understand the landforms and landscapes shown on OS maps.

▼ Figure 2: Identifying slopes and landforms using contour lines

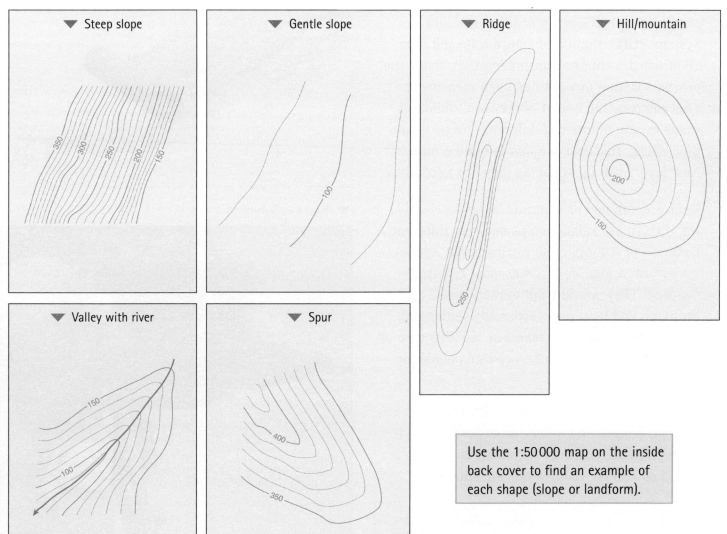

Use the 1:50 000 map on the inside back cover to find an example of each shape (slope or landform).

The future for maps and map making

There are many different types of maps made today, for a wide variety of purposes. Some of these are for general use. Others are highly specialised for specific purposes. Some of the measurements are still made on the ground by **surveyors** [Figure 2]. As computers have become faster and more powerful, measurements in the form of digital data are increasingly collected remotely by satellites. The data is then used to create maps.

Geographic Information Systems (GIS)

Maps using computers and digital data are produced using Geographical Information Systems (**GIS**). Computers store collected data, all of which contains information that 'fixes' the precise location of what has been measured. This could be the height of the land, buildings, roads or any number of different things. It can then check, find and use this to build a map. New layers can be added as they are needed.

Data is combined as separate layers to clearly see if there are relationships between different factors. For example, the Environment Agency may want to identify areas at most risk from flooding. They would want to map relief, drainage and land use – especially settlement. Insurance companies would also use this type of map to decide how much to charge people for house insurance.

GIS can also be used together with photos, satellite images and other resources to provide even more information. An added advantage is that they can be updated quickly and easily.

Think of two or three other groups or organisations who might find GIS useful. What sort of data would they use GIS to show?

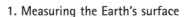
▼ Figure 1: GIS maps

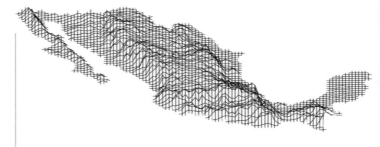
1. Measuring the Earth's surface

3. Adding detail to the land surface

▼ Figure 2: Surveying

2. Making a terrain model

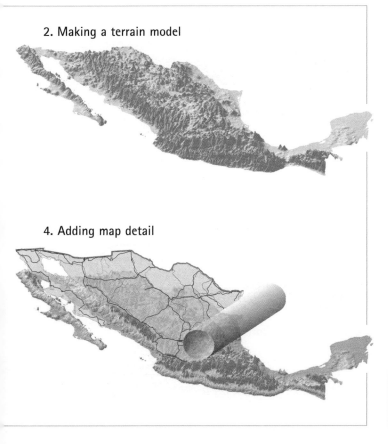

4. Adding map detail

Global Positioning Systems (GPS)

GPS allow you to find out exactly where you are on the Earth's surface. They work by comparing the timed signals from three or more satellites. At the moment they can locate where someone is to within 100 metres. Uses for GPS include:

- small, portable devices used by walkers, climbers and sailors. These help them navigate accurately in remote areas such as deserts, mountains and oceans.

- in-car navigation systems use GPS to provide detailed information about the best route to take. This can be updated and changed as road and traffic conditions change. It helps drivers avoid road works, accidents and traffic jams.

What groups of users would find GPS helpful to them in their work? Explain why.

Figure 3: A car fitted with a GPS device

3·1 Who are you?

Geographers investigate 'big questions' or ideas. For example: why do people live in certain places? How and why do different people live the way they do?

Why do some people see things differently to me?

What influences the way I see the world?

Why do I live where I do?

Where does my food come from?

How does where I live affect me and my life?

Who makes the clothes I wear?

Why are some people rich and some people poor?

▲ Figure 1: Who are you?

▼ Figure 2: The world according to Shazney

The World According to Shazney

In **Figure 2**, Shazney describes her own **personal geographies.** Even though geography might seem just a school subject like any other, as individuals we each have our own personal geographies. These geographies come from the variety of experiences that we each have. They include where we live now, where we grew up, where our families are from, and where we spend our time. Your personal geography is even influenced by the TV programmes you watch and the music you listen to. It is shaped by all the places with which you have daily contact.

Read the text in **Figure 2**. What would you choose to say about yourself?

'My world is my family and friends. I live in Colindale in northwest London. Colindale is the centre of my world. But when I go down the road to buy food, magazines, music and clothes, many of them come from different countries around the world. I learn about the world from things I buy and use, from my family, friends and others I meet. Many of my friends speak more than one language. At school we celebrate lots of cultural festivals and learn about the different ways people live their lives. I enjoy this because it makes me think about the world in a different way.

'I was born in London and both my parents were born in Britain; but my ancestors come from all over the globe. I'm a bit French, Turkish, Scottish, Russian Jewish and Romany Gipsy, so my identity is all of these. I see myself as a Londoner as well as being English, British and European.

'At weekends sometimes I go camping and climbing, or I might go with my family to Wales or Scotland where there are mountains and great beaches. As well as Britain, I've travelled around Europe on holiday and can speak some French and Spanish. When I'm older I hope to learn more languages and travel across the world.'

We often behave differently in different places or with different people. This is because we all have our own **identities** about certain places which can be strong or weak.

> Make a mind map, or spider diagram, showing your personal geographies – all your connections with different places, both near and far away.

A very British meal?

You can't get more British than fish and chips [Figure 3] and a cup of tea – or can you? You might be surprised by the possible origin of fish and chips. They were first sold in London's Docklands when it was an important arrival point for people coming to England. The chips came from the Huguenot community, originally from France, where they were called *pommes frites*. Fried fish was a speciality of the Jewish community which settled in the East End of London. It may then have been the Irish community in London who put the two together.

Our 'traditional' cup of tea typically uses tea leaves from India and sugar from the Caribbean. So, something we consider very British is actually a mixture from lots of different countries and cultures. Even fish and chips and a cup of tea have **multiple identities**.

▼ Figure 3: The Great British fish and chips?

3·2 Links and connections

*'No man is an island entire
of itself'* John Donne (1593-1631)

This quotation is from the author
and philosopher John Donne who
lived four hundred years ago. Even
then there was an understanding
that none of us can exist without
having connections with other
people and places. We are all
connected to each other, but in
different ways. Our connections
could be through our families and
their past experiences, or through
things we buy and **consume**.

Look at **Figure 1**. Do you know
where your breakfast came from?
Who made your clothes? How does
your email and post get transported
and delivered? Who made the
technology you use? Who keeps it
running smoothly?

▲ **Figure 1: 'No man is an island'.** In all our everyday activities
we connect with other people

Geography is all about connections and how
these shape our experiences of the world. We all
play a part in the experiences that other people
have of the world.

Britain's global connections

In the past, people were more dependent on
where they lived for their knowledge and
experience of the world. Life in Britain was
influenced by different cultures from the rest of
Europe. European goods, ideas and beliefs were
already found in Britain long before travel to
other countries became commonplace. The
Romans, Vikings, Picts, Celts, Anglo-Saxons and
Normans all came to or invaded Britain.

As technology developed, new links were made
with places further away. New transport
systems, e.g. canals, roads and railways, helped
places in the UK to become better connected.
More recently, ships and aeroplanes have meant
that people are able to travel **internationally** to
experience the world. Mobile phones, satellite
systems and the internet have all made the
world appear to be getting smaller.

Links and connections are not experienced equally by everyone. Both in historical times and today, trade often benefits the more powerful groups, countries or companies the most.

Trade is just one way that Britain and all the world's countries are connected to other places. In **Figure 2**, there are two maps, one showing which countries the UK traded with in the first century AD, and the larger map showing the main countries the UK trades with today. What are the main differences that you can spot between them?

Sir Walter Raleigh (1552-1618), explorer in the times of Queen Elizabeth I said:

'Whosoever commands the trade of the world commands the riches of the world and henceforth the world itself.'

Figure 2: Trade routes in the first century AD and today
Trade is just one way in which the UK and other countries are connected

Figure 2a: Trade routes in the first century AD ▶

▼ Figure 2b: The UK's main trading partners today

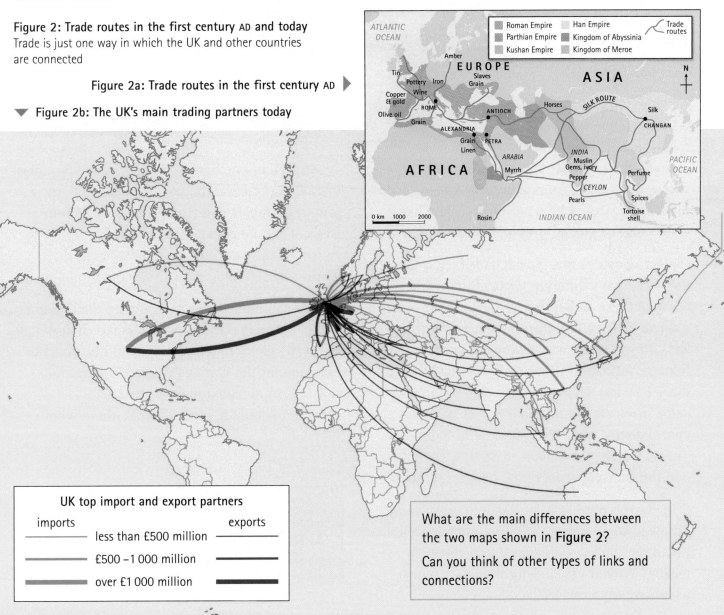

UK top import and export partners

imports	exports
less than £500 million	
£500 – 1 000 million	
over £1 000 million	

What are the main differences between the two maps shown in **Figure 2**?

Can you think of other types of links and connections?

3·3 Local ... or global?

▼ Figure 1: The global chocolate bar

Paper from Norway

Art and Design work from the UK

Wrapper printed in Indonesia

Foil made in Slough

Transported by a company from Stockton-on-Tees

Cocoa from Ghana

Sugar from Guatemala

Vegetable fat from Germany

Many of the things you buy, even from your local shops, don't come from your local area or even the UK. For example, a bar of chocolate has a wide range of global links and connections.

Figure 1 shows how a typical bar of chocolate can link with many different parts of the world. Some of these global connections are necessary – cocoa needs a hot, tropical climate to grow well, so you won't find it growing on farms in Kent or Yorkshire! Other global connections are there because it can be much cheaper to make some products in other places. For example, the chocolate bar wrapper is printed in Indonesia. This is the cheapest place to do this, even if you add the transport cost of the finished wrappers.

Why do you think it is so cheap to make some things in some places? Why are some goods, like bread and milk, usually produced relatively locally? Why are some chocolate bars more expensive than others?

When a company decides where to buy products or raw materials from, cost is usually the most important factor. If a country has low **labour** costs, it can be cheaper to build a factory there. However, transporting the goods across the world can pollute and harm the environment.

Should companies take this into account? Some people think that if companies make choices that harm the environment, they should be taxed to make up for the damage caused. Others think that it is up to **consumers** to make environmentally-friendly choices about what they buy.

Choose five things that you've recently bought or had bought for you. What were each made from? Where was each made? What are the home countries of the companies which sold them?

Key Words: labour, see page 124

Think global... act local

▼ Figure 2: Lee's story

'In school, we did some lessons on the impact that our lives can have upon other places. Since then I've thought a lot about where my food comes from, and the footprint that my life leaves on the planet. When we go shopping, my mum and I always try to buy food that was produced locally - this helps local farmers and causes less pollution as the food doesn't have to travel so far. I've also persuaded my family to change to environmentally-friendly washing powder. It still does the job but without causing so much damage to the environment.

'We also recycle as much as we can at home. We've introduced three recycling bins in the kitchen and keep our other waste separate. When we go to the supermarket we return our empty glass bottles, cans and paper for recycling. These are only small things and on their own they won't make a big difference, but together they will.'

▼ Figure 3: A supermarket recycling centre

Many supermarkets have recycling bins for paper, glass, plastic, old clothes and aluminium

▼ Figure 4: Recycling bins for home collection

In **Figure 2**, Lee talks about where the things she and her family use come from and how this has changed some of the choices they make when shopping. Buying from local producers, for example from farm shops or farmer's markets, not only helps local farmers and the local economy, it reduces transport costs and pollution. Her family also **recycle** waste by taking it to local recycling centres [**Figure 3**]. Many councils now collect waste for recycling from our homes [**Figure 4**].

All these actions help you think about your role as a **global citizen**. Choosing to recycle waste can have an impact on your local area (such as local waste disposal sites); also by recycling plastic you can reduce the pollution that affects our rivers and seas.

Lee and her family have made small changes in their lives to create less damage to the environment. Do you think it is worth the effort? What other actions could they could take?

Key Words: recycle, see page 124

3·4   What is globalisation?

Figure 1: Where is this photo taken?

The word **globalisation** is used frequently on the television, radio and in newspapers – but what does it mean?

If you find it difficult to describe globalisation, then you are not the only one! People disagree about what it means, and whether it is good or bad. Most conclude that really it is neither.

To many people, globalisation means 'spreading across the globe'. With global use of the internet and worldwide availability of products and services from **Trans National Companies (TNCs)** such as Coca-Cola, Nike, McDonalds and Manchester United, you can now enjoy many of the same things wherever you are in the world.

Many people see it as a positive thing that will help many countries to become more economically developed and successful, like the USA and other wealthy countries.

> Write down some ideas of what you think globalisation might mean.

Figure 2: What globalisation means

The internet can be a good thing, but most of it is in English, and some places don't have reliable electricity and phones so not everyone can get it. I think that we're wrong when we think that everyone will be affected by globalisation. Some places will but many others won't!

I think globalisation is a great thing. If it means that successful companies can spread to other places and employ more and more people, then everyone will get richer: so everyone benefits.

If globalisation really exists then why don't companies from other countries, apart from Europe and the USA, build factories in my local town?

Globalisation means that people all over the world have access to a vast range of food and products.

Key Words: globalisation, Trans National Companies (TNCs) see page 124

Other people think globalisation really means global domination by the rich and powerful. They view it as a negative force that either will make everywhere the same, or will make the rich countries even richer, and the poor countries poorer. They point out that most of the TNCs are owned by **More Economically Developed Countries (MEDCs)** that make all the profit.

What is clear, despite the debates, is that globalisation is a very important process which affects everyone.

Globalisation and conflict

For some people, globalisation can mean conflict. On the news we often hear of wars, or demonstrations where local people are fighting to get their views heard.

Figure 3 shows a woman arguing with police about her access to water. The Bolivian government tried to sell the country's water to a private American company. Local people were worried that this would raise the price of water. But some Americans argued that their experience in managing water would help them to do a better job than the Bolivian government.

Globalisation doesn't always mean conflict. Look back at **Figure 1**. Where did you think the photograph was taken? It is actually an area of Singapore, looking towards Arab Street, where most of the locals are from Arabic countries. They settled in Singapore and redesigned it using Arabic influences. It is now a tourist hot-spot and a favourite place for other Singaporeans to shop and eat. Globalisation can therefore mean bringing the world to your doorstep.

> Can you find examples in your local area of global connections?

▼ Figure 3: Protests in Bolivia, South America, 2001

> Why can't globalisation mean people co-operating and supporting each other, with shared aims to improve life for everyone?

> Why do there have to be more powerful countries and less powerful ones?

> Which opinions in **Figure 2** do you agree with and why? What additional information would you need to be sure?

3·5 Changing ways

One of the problems with globalisation is our easy access to resources across the world. If we keep using global resources like water and oil at our present rate, soon there will not be enough for everyone and they will eventually run out. The Earth cannot keep pace with people consuming more and more of its resources. This is especially true of **non-renewable resources** like oil.

▼ Figure 1: Sustainable energy production: wind turbines in Anglesey, Wales
The UK government has promised that by 2010 10 per cent of the UK's electricity will be produced from renewable sources like windpower.

aGeographers have helped to try to find different ways for people to improve their quality of life without causing so much harm to the environment. These methods are often referred to as **sustainable**. They allow the Earth to renew resources to replace those being used. Such schemes can also improve people's quality of life, so are examples of what we call **sustainable development**.

Greenwich Community Food Co-operative

The Greenwich Community Food Co-operative is a fruit and vegetable co-operative society, based in London. It takes fresh produce to local residents. The society gives fruit to local people in exchange for a small payment. Any profit goes back into the scheme.

The scheme aims to ensure that people in low-income areas receive a balanced diet. A more healthy population should help to improve the area for everyone. Links have also been created with nearby market farmers. They can then sell their goods locally without the cost of transporting them long distances.

▼ Figure 2: Unsustainable energy production

Key Words: non-renewable , sustainable see page 124

Figure 3: This newsletter tells you about a LETS scheme

Something for nothing?

Travelling around the world
for free

In Greenwich, London, LETS can be used in local community colleges so people can take up courses to learn new skills and gain qualifications.

Sounds too good to be true? Well, that's exactly what James Taris has done. He is part of a new breed of organisation that lets people trade their skills with each other without using money.

Local Exchange Trading Systems (LETS) schemes are an alternative to paying for goods and services with money. People trade their skills for other people's skills in order to get necessary tasks completed. Such systems are proving increasingly successful as they allow people to support each other and play a part in the local community without being dependent on money to pay for the transactions. Instead, people 'bank' LETS points that they can then use when they need a service in the future.

'I have three children and a disabled partner. It's tough at times but through LETS I get help with the children, household repairs and shopping. In return my partner does ironing when able and I make cakes for special occasions.'

Unlike a direct swap, people signed up to a LETS scheme can trade with anyone in the scheme. They trade when they want to and at their own pace. Payment is made in LETS 'units', not money.

It isn't just the local community which benefits from LETS schemes. Such trading systems are being set up all over the world. One LETS Greenwich member writes:

'I am a member of 'Waterfront LETS' in Greenwich and loving it! There are LETS all over the world: Canada, America, Australia, Argentina, Holland … just to mention a few. Similar schemes in other countries have different titles and currencies, but all with the same aims. Arrangements between people, to exchange goods and services, creates a pooled system of credits and debits. This builds a local scheme of currencies which results in a stronger community.'

Find out if there is a LETS scheme in your local area. How does it work?

 **3·6** # Globalisation: past, present and future

People have always wondered what the future would be like. Will everyone have enough food, water and other resources? What will be the next big invention or piece of technology? The photos here show how some people in the past imagined life might be in the twenty-first century. How accurate were they?

The science fiction series *Star Trek* [Figure 1] was first shown on TV in the 1960s. It gives one idea of how people thought we would live and dress in the year 2000 – with regular travel between planets in space. Looking at **Figure 1** and **2** it is hard to believe that people thought we would be wearing clothes like this – but they did. In the 1960s and 70s, everyone was excited about space travel. They imagined that this was how people might live in the future.

Space travel also changed people's perception of the world, especially the first pictures of the Earth from space.

Look at the images from *Star Trek*. What predictions did the programme makers get right?

▼ Figure 2: Beam me up: a new way to travel?

▼ Figure 1: The crew of the Starship Enterprise

▲ Figure 3: An image from the film *1984* showing Big Brother

In 1948, George Orwell wrote *1984*, a novel sugesting what life might be like in that year. The story was very bleak. Everyone was watched by their TV screens, which were under the control of Big Brother (this is where the name of the TV show came from). The idea was that we might all, one day, be under constant surveillance. Already this is true in many towns and cities today, where CCTV can monitor all our movements.

In Orwell's book, there was constant war between the world's major powers. The government controlled what people wore, said and even thought, with strict rules and very severe punishments.

George Orwell didn't intend his story to be a prediction, but a warning of what the future could be like. He included harsh punishments such as being sent to Room 101 – a room that contained your worst fears. Although nobody would say that Orwell's vision has come true today, some people do think that governments and other organisations have too much control over our daily lives.

> Think of another book or TV series which you know quite well from the past and which looked at the future. List the things which have come true.

Why think about the future?

Why are geographers interested in the future? In the news we often see or hear frightening predictions about the future. For instance, global warming might affect our climate and the way millions of people, plants and animals live. Or we might run out of oil and other non-renewable resources.

On a positive note, technology is changing our lives all the time. Research into new medicines may eventually control or cure once-fatal diseases.

These predictions may or may not come true. Geographers are interested in them, however, because they want to try to prevent disasters happening. They are also looking for ways to improve the quality of people's lives.

> What is your vision of the future? What do you think the world will be like in fifty years time?

Our global future

Past predictions

On pages 32–33 you looked at how George Orwell, the author of the book *1984*, and the makers of the sci-fi series *Star Trek*, thought the future might be like.

- Copy and complete **Figure 1** to show how many of the predictions made in *Star Trek* and *1984* have or have not come true.

- Add a list of new things which exist now, but were not predicted.

▼ Figure 1: Predictions ... which of these has come true?

What was accurately predicted?	What hasn't come true?	List some of the things which have happened but were not predicted
	people wearing silver all the time	mobile phones
	food pills	internet

A global Britain

In a recent survey it was found that the most popular food in the UK was chicken tikka masala. In the 1960s very few people in the UK would have heard of this. It is a good everyday example of how globalisation has affected the present, with people regularly choosing to eat food dishes from all over the world.

- Talk to your grandparents or other people who remember life in the 1950s and 60s. When they were young, how did they imagine life in the twenty-first century?

Your current observations

Now look back at your completed table. Use it to help you make a list of:

- aspects of life which have not changed since the 1950s

- aspects which have changed.

Try to explain why some things have stayed the same and why others have changed.

Your future predictions

- What are the most powerful influences that might change our lives in the future? It might help you to think about what influences you now:

    - what you choose to wear and eat
    - how you spend your time
    - what current technology is fashionable.

- What might life be like in fifty years' time? Use the Mind Map [Figure 2] to help organise your ideas.

▼ Figure 2: Mind Map

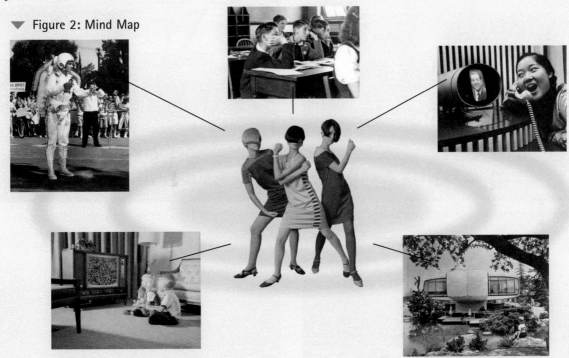

Prioritise your ideas

Look back at all your ideas and predictions:

- Which of your ideas would you like to happen?

- Put your ideas in order – the ones you think are most likely to happen at the top and least likely to happen at the bottom.

Organising your ideas

- Use your ideas to describe what a school of the future may be like. (You might wish to adapt the work you did on pages 8 and 9.) Use drawings, plans, photos and text to create your future school. Will *all* schools look like this?

4·1 Types of settlement

About 30 per cent of the Earth's surface is land. Of this, it is only possible to live comfortably on about 12 per cent. The rest is unsuitable – it is too hot, too cold, too dry, too wet, too steep or covered by forest. The world's population of over six billion have settled unevenly over the suitable land.

Types of settlements

A settlement is a place where people have decided to live or settle. People live in many different types of settlements. A settlement can be any size, from a single **isolated dwelling** to a **city**.

▼ Figure 1: A village in Namibia, southern Africa

About two-thirds of Namibians live in villages in rural areas

▼ Figure 2: Shanty town in Peru, South America

Life is often difficult in these temporary settlements

▼ Figure 3: Tokyo skyline

Japan's capital is one of the world's largest cities

▼ Figure 4: Bedouin tent, Wadi Rum, Jordan

The Bedouin are nomads, moving their tents and animals from place to place

Some people live in **rural** settlements, like the village in Namibia [Figure 1]. In 2000, 69 per cent of Namibian's lived in rural areas like this. However, the **United Nations** (**UN**) predicts that this will fall to 57 per cent by 2020. Patterns are changing as rural dwellers **migrate** to **urban** areas in search of jobs and better facilities. In **Less Economically Developed Countries** (**LEDCs**) many begin by living in temporary settlements called **shanty towns** [Figure 2] on the edge of a city. Many MEDCs already have higher urban populations. In Japan, 65 per cent already live in urban areas [Figure 3]. By 2020 this is likely to reach 70 per cent.

> What do you think the urban-rural split of the UK's population is? Find out.

Some people move from place to place all the time. These are **nomadic** people, living in tents or caravans, such as the Bedouin people of the Middle East [Figure 4] and travellers found throughout central Europe.

Site and situation

When we describe the location of a settlement, we usually look at both its **site** and its **situation**.

- The **site** of a settlement is a description of the land the settlement is built on; for example, whether it is on flat or sloping land and its height above sea level.

- The **situation** is a description of the area surrounding the settlement. It could include the name, direction and distance away from other settlements and physical features such as woodlands, hills, rivers or the sea.

A good way to remember these terms is that site is a small word and it describes a small area, whilst situation is a bigger word and describes a larger area.

> (A) flat land that is easy to build on and farm
> (B) fertile soil for farming
> (C) a fresh water supply for drinking, washing, cooking and watering crops
> (D) an easily defendable site, such as a hill or river meander
> (E) building materials such as wood or stone
> (F) wood for fuel
> (G) raw materials to make implements e.g. clay or iron ore

▼ Figure 5: A perfect location for building a settlement

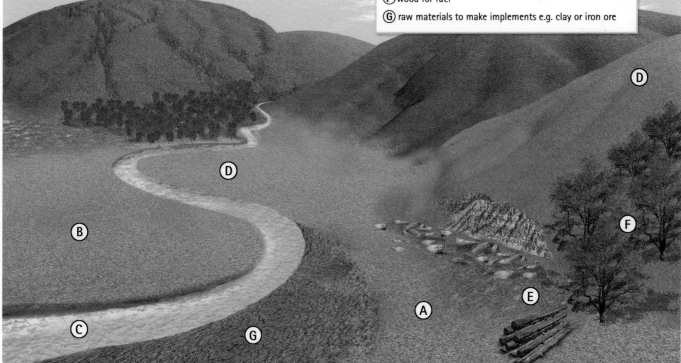

Settlement: growth and functions

Why settlements grow

Many factors influence where a settlement starts and grows. In the past, physical factors were extremely important. People would have looked for locations that had some or all of the features shown in **Figure 5** on page 37.

Today, human factors are becoming increasingly important in locating settlements. **Figure 1** shows the effects of some physical and human factors on settlement location.

Government policies also often affect whether settlements grow or not. For example, it is very difficult to get permission to build on areas of **green belt** around major UK cities. This means they cannot grow outwards – a problem when new housing is needed.

▼ Figure 1: The factors that influence the location of a settlement

	Factor	Description	Example
Physical	Defensive site	Built in a river meander or on a hill to protect it from enemy attack	Durham, Northumberland
	Wet or spring line site	Next to a spring in an otherwise dry area, such as chalk	Bexleyhill, West Sussex
	Dry island site	On a dry spot in an otherwise wet area, such as marshland	Ely, Cambridgeshire
	Bridging point	At a narrow point on a river, or at a place with a firm bed and banks for building a bridge	London
	Gap town	In or near a gap through a range of hills or mountains	Dorking, Surrey
	Natural resources	On fertile soil, or near raw materials such as coal, iron ore, etc.	Ebbw Vale, South Wales
Human	Route centre (node)	At an accessible place where roads or railways meet, such as a market town in a farming area	Aylesbury, Buckinghamshire
	New Town	The government plans New Towns to remove people from overcrowded cities	East Kilbride, near Glasgow
	Self-help schemes	To replace shanty towns, the government provides suitable land, water and electricity supplies and cheap building materials	Mumbai (Bombay) in India

> What are the main factors that influenced the location of the settlement you live in? Are they mainly physical, human or an equal mixture of both?

Settlement functions

Most settlements have a variety of **functions**, offering particular services to the people that live there or nearby. A settlement's functions depend on the physical and human factors that caused it to be located there, and those that have affected it while it has grown.

Figure 2 shows some examples of settlements that have different functions. Some larger settlements may have more than one function. London has many functions. As well as being a capital city, it is a port, a financial centre, a tourist centre, a university city, a route centre and an administrative centre.

▼ Figure 2: Settlement functions

Function	Example
Port	Portsmouth, Hampshire
Industrial town	Sheffield, South Yorkshire
Market town	Hereford, Herefordshire
University town	Cambridge, Cambridgeshire
Dormitory town	Crowthorne, Berkshire
Tourist resort	Skegness, Lincolnshire
Cathedral city	York, North Yorkshire

> Think about the settlement you live in. What function(s) does it have?

Settlement hierarchy

Settlements have different population sizes. From smallest to largest they are: isolated dwelling, hamlet, village, town and city. Putting things in order of importance is known as a **hierarchy**. Can you place the people who work in your school into a hierarchy? (The Head Teacher would be at the top.)

▼ Figure 3: A settlement hierarchy

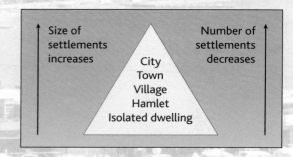

Size of settlements increases | Number of settlements decreases

City
Town
Village
Hamlet
Isolated dwelling

▼ Figure 4: Settlement sizes

Type of settlement	Population range	Examples from the West Midlands
City	>100 000	Wolverhampton 236 582
Town	2001–100 000	Bridgnorth 52 497
Village	51–2000	Ditton Priors 1 557
Hamlet	Up to 50	Upper Netchwood 25

Figure 3 shows that there are many more small settlements than larger ones. As size increases, the number of settlements decreases. **Figure 4** gives a rough guide to the population of different size settlements in the UK. The size at which a village becomes a town is not exact. The range of services and facilities is also important. As settlements become larger they offer more services. A hamlet may have no services, or may have limited services such as a post box and phone box. A city will have many services of many different types.

> Make a list of the different services for a town and a village in your home area. What extra facilities are found in the nearest large city?

Key Words: functions, hierarchy see page 124

4·3 Settlement shapes

There are three main types of settlements found in rural areas: dispersed, nucleated and linear.

1 Dispersed settlements

These are isolated dwellings – buildings on their own, such as farms or country houses scattered around an area [Figure 1]. There are a number of isolated dwellings away from the main settlement in Figure 3a. Can you find Langtree House and Payables Farm?

2 Nucleated settlements

These have a compact shape [Figure 2], usually because they have grown up around a central point (nucleus) such as a crossroads, T-junction, or maybe a village green or pond. Figures 3a and 3b show a good example: Woodcote, northwest of Reading in Berkshire.

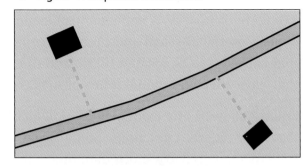

▼ Figure 1: dispersed settlements

▼ Figure 2: a nucleated settlement

▼ Figure 3a: A nucleated settlement

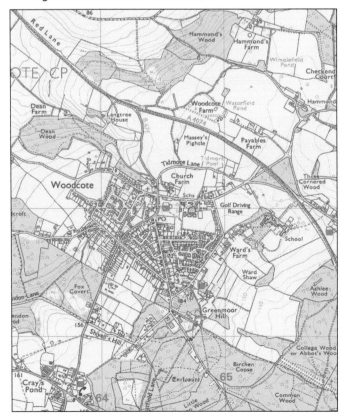

OS map of Woodcote

▼ Figure 3b: A nucleated settlement

Aerial photo of Woodcote

3 Linear settlements

These are long and thin in shape [Figure 4]. They have developed along a communication route, usually a road, but sometimes a river or canal. Figures 5a and 5b show a good example: Stoke Row, northwest of Reading in Berkshire.

▼ Figure 4: The shape of a linear settlement

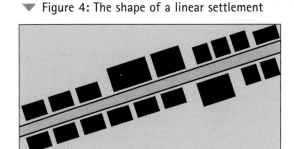

▼ Figure 5a: A linear settlement

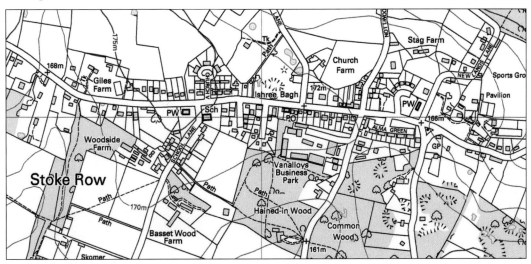

OS map of Stoke Row

▼ Figure 5b: A linear settlement

Aerial photo of Stoke Row

It is fairly easy to recognise these types and shapes in rural areas, especially on Ordnance Survey maps and aerial photographs. However, as nearby towns and cities expand outwards, or as rural settlements grow themselves, they start to merge into a larger urban area and become harder to identify.

> Can you find examples of an isolated, a nucleated and a linear settlement in a rural area close to your school? Use an Ordnance Survey (OS) map to help you.

4·4 Services and shopping

Settlements of different sizes offer different types and numbers of **services** [Figure 1]. A small settlement offers only **low order** services such as a post office or general store, and has shops selling low order goods, for example bread, milk and newspapers. A large settlement has low order services as well as many **high order** services and shops selling high order goods, for example jewellery.

> What services are offered to you by the settlement you live in?

What decides the services that are offered?

Shops require a certain number of customers to make a profit. This number is called a **threshold**. The population of Ditton Priors is only 1 557. This is not a big enough threshold for companies like McDonalds or Marks & Spencer to locate there [Figure 1].

A settlement with a large **sphere of influence** attracts shoppers from many other settlements. Bridgnorth may only have a population of 52 497, but it attracts shoppers from the surrounding rural area. It therefore has a higher threshold which encourages some higher order shops and services to set up there [Figure 1].

A shopping hierarchy

Shopping centres can be placed in a hierarchy [Figure 2]. Figure 3 shows examples of different types of shops.

▼ Figure 1: Services in selected settlements in the West Midlands

Name of settlement	Services offered
Upper Netchwood (25)	Phone box, telephone box, disused chapel
Ditton Priors (1 557)	Church, general store, public house/restaurant/hotel, petrol station/garage, butchers, doctor's surgery, village hall, post office, primary school, tea room, museum
Bridgnorth (52 497)	A wide range of chain stores, e.g. Woolworths, Sainsburys, Boots and WH Smith. Higher order services, e.g. two secondary schools and country hospital. Higher order shops, e.g. jewellers, opticians and furniture shops.
Wolverhampton (236 582)	Multiple examples of all the services offered in Bridgnorth. Higher order services, e.g. university and department store. Wider range of shops for comparison shopping. A main line railway station and bus station.

▼ Figure 2: A shopping hierarchy

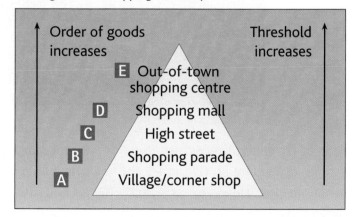

Key Words: services, low order, high order, threshold, sphere of influence see page 124

▼ Figure 3: Types of shops and shopping centres

A A village shop, or a corner shop in an urban area, sells mainly low order goods to a small threshold population from the local area. It often opens seven days a week and long hours each day.

B A shopping parade is a few shops along a road. They are found in the **suburbs** of a town or city and serve people from the local area, as well as passing trade. They include: a small supermarket, take-away restaurants, an off-licence, a video/DVD library, a hairdressers and a sub-post office. There may be off-road parking.

C The high street of a **Central Business District CBD** has a wider range of shops, more high order services, and is the main road through the centre of a town. It has car parks and caters for people from all over the town and from the surrounding area.

D **Shopping malls** are found in larger towns and cities. They are indoor shopping centres, on two or more floors. As well as a wide range of comparison shops and a multi-storey car park, there may be a cinema, many cafés and restaurants and perhaps even a crèche, making it a place where people will want to spend the day.

E An out-of-town shopping centre can be a large indoor shopping centre, containing many shops, or a site with a number of warehouses selling electrical goods, DIY, furniture, carpets and similar goods. Both usually have large car parks surrounding them. They are often located on the edge of urban areas close to a motorway junction, ring road or main route out of town.

Key Words: Central Business District (CBD) see page 124

Shopping has changed a great deal in the last fifty years. One of the main reasons has been the increase in car use and ownership. People can now travel easily to large shopping centres many miles from their home.

The growth of out-of-town shopping centres has meant that smaller town centres have suffered from a lack of customers and many shops have gone out of business. A sign that this has happened to a shopping centre is the number of empty shops, or shops now being used by charities.

Traditional corner shops have begun to close down, as people prefer shops with a wider variety of goods for sale. Goods in corner shops also tend to be more expensive than in larger chain stores. Recently, the major supermarket chains have begun to develop their own 'corner shops', replacing them with stores like Tesco Metro that are open long hours and sell goods at low prices.

> Do you have a corner shop near you, or has a store like a Tesco Metro replaced it?

Many traditional high streets have become **pedestrianised**. No traffic is allowed, apart from cleaning trucks and emergency vehicles. They may have benches, flowers, trees and even street entertainers. **Figures 1a** and **1b** show the high street in Guildford, Surrey, before and after pedestrianisation.

▼ Figure 1a: Guildford high street before pedestrianisation

▼ Figure 1b: The same high street after pedestrianisation

> What advantages do you think the pedestrianised street has for shoppers?

▼ Investigation

Shops and services in rural areas

▼ Figure 2: Sketch map of Woodleigh and Bourneham

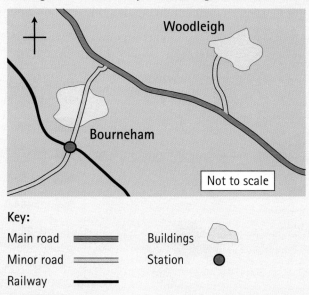

Key:

Main road	▬▬▬▬
Minor road	═════
Railway	▬▬▬▬
Buildings	(shape)
Station	●

Look at the two villages of Woodleigh and Bourneham shown in **Figure 2**.

They are roughly the same size and fairly close to each other.

In Bourneham you can buy a three bedroom house for £180 000, yet in Woodleigh a six bedroom house costs £230 000. **Why doesn't the bigger house cost a lot more?**

In Woodleigh there is only a primary school and a pub. In Bourneham there is a butchers, pub, village shop, post office and a primary school. It is also near a railway station with four trains to a large city every hour during peak times.

- From the list below, decide what new shop or service would be most useful to people in Woodleigh.

- Rank them in order of importance (most important first):
    - newsagent
    - post office
    - bakery with café
    - grocer
    - playschool group
    - bank

- Explain why you picked the top three shops or services. For each one, who would benefit most – young or old people, retired people, young families or commuters?

- What might happen to Bourneham if a large supermarket was built next to the railway station? Draw a table and use it to list the advantages and disadvantages to Bourneham of building the supermarket.

- The primary schools in both villages are in danger of closing because of falling numbers. If they close, the remaining children will have to catch the school bus at 7.30 each morning to travel to school in a nearby town.

- Write a letter to the Chief Education Officer of the Local Education Authority to say why you think either (or both) schools should be kept open. You can write the letter as a pupil, a local parent or as one of the head teachers.

4·6 Urban growth

The world's urban areas are growing rapidly – a process called **urbanisation**. By 2001, approximately 48 per cent of the world's population lived in urban areas. **Figure 1** shows the urban population for each country.

▼ Figure 1: World urban population

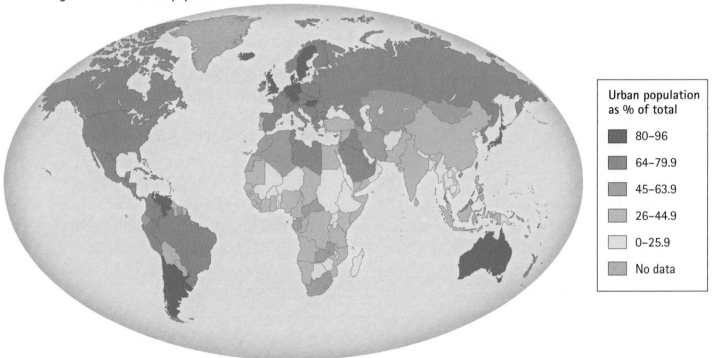

Urban population as % of total

■	80–96
■	64–79.9
■	45–63.9
■	26–44.9
☐	0–25.9
■	No data

To begin with, urban growth was due to **rural-urban migration** – people moving from the countryside to towns and cities. However, the major cause today is **natural increase**.

Natural increase is calculated by subtracting the number of deaths per year from the number of births per year. A positive figure means that the birth rate is higher than the death rate. Natural increase is thought to account for 60 per cent of urban growth, and migration for 40 per cent.

International migration also affects urban growth. In 1999, 150 million people lived outside their country of origin.

Natural increase is generally higher in LEDCs than in MEDCs. There are many reasons for this including:
- high birth rates due to lack of access to birth control
- a decreasing death rate due to improvements in health services.

As natural increase tends to be higher in LEDCs, these countries have the highest rates of urban growth. Between 1950 and 1990, the total population of Asia doubled, and the urban population tripled.

In some MEDCs urban populations are growing very slowly because many city dwellers are moving to the countryside. This is called **counter-urbanisation**.

Key Words: urbanisation, rural–urban migration, natural increase, international migration, counter-urbanisation see page 124

Push and pull factors

There are many reasons for rural-urban migration. They can be divided into push and pull factors. A **push factor** is something negative that makes people want to move out of the countryside. A **pull factor** is something positive that makes people want to live in cities [Figure 2].

> Look carefully at the push and pull factors in **Figure 2**.
>
> Try to identify some of these factors in **Figures 3** and **4**. Can you think of any others?

Figure 2: Some push and pull factors for rural-urban migration

Natural disasters
Rural poverty
Low crop yields
Lack of services
Job opportunities
Better quality of life
Bright lights
Access to services

Figure 3: A rural area in an LEDC

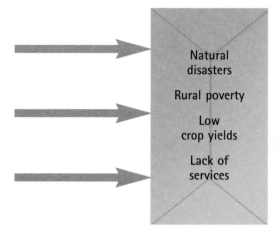

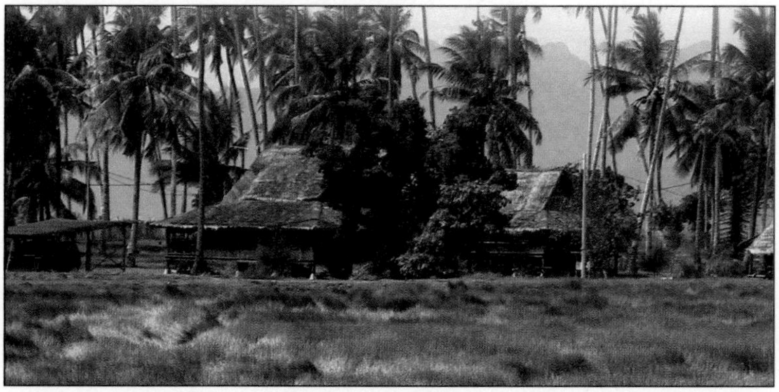

A village on the island of Langkawi, Malaysia

Figure 4: An urban area in an LEDC

DENTAL SURGERY
AVON
HOT WOK

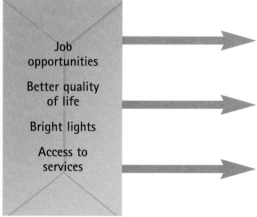

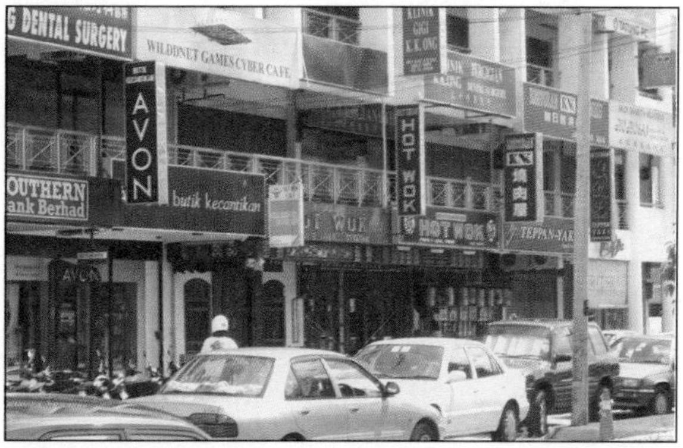

A street in Georgetown, capital of Penang, Malaysia

Most of the world's major cities are also centres of international trade and employment. This makes cities attractive places to live, because of greater job opportunities. More jobs, greater access to health care and education are all major pull factors. There is also the pull of the 'bright lights' in a city, for example theatres and restaurants.

Young men are more likely to migrate to cities than women or other age groups. The rural areas they leave behind can suffer with an aged population unable to look after the land properly, and families with no fathers.

> List the reasons why you might prefer to live in a city instead of the countryside. Would everyone feel the same as you? If not, why might they feel differently? Think about the effect that age, gender and personal history might have.

Key Words: push factor, pull factor see page 124

Land use in towns and cities in MEDCs

In 1925 a sociologist called Burgess produced a simple model (the concentric zone model) to describe different areas of land use in Chicago. He noticed that land use changed as you moved away from the Central Business District, or CBD. Geographers often use this model to try fit today's towns and cities [Figure 1].

▼ Figure 1: The concentric zone model

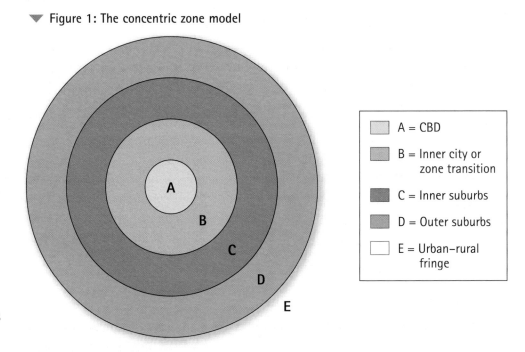

A = CBD

B = Inner city or zone transition

C = Inner suburbs

D = Outer suburbs

E = Urban–rural fringe

Lincoln is a typical British city. It is the county town of Lincolnshire and in the 2001 Census it had a population of 85 595. Like many cities, it has distinctive land use zones. The following photos [Figures 2 to 6] show Lincoln.

Central Business District (CBD)

This was originally the most accessible part of a city, where the main roads met. Today there is often a ring road around the CBD to cut down traffic congestion. Railway and bus stations are often in the CBD. Being the most accessible zone with the largest number of potential customers, large shops want to locate there [Figure 2]. This has resulted in high land prices – and tall buildings as it is cheaper to build upwards, taking up less space. Offices, public buildings, cinemas, theatres and restaurants are common in the CBD.

▼ Figure 2: Lincoln's CBD

▼ Figure 3: Lincoln's inner city

Inner city

Around the CBD is the **inner city** area [Figure 3]. It is also called the 'zone in transition' because it has experienced a lot of change. In the nineteenth century it usually contained factories as well as the **terraced** houses that the factory workers lived in, plus corner shops to serve them. The houses have small back yards. When they were first built they had no kitchen, bathroom or central heating.

Many of the old inner city factories have now been demolished or converted into apartments. Some terraced houses have been modernised, or knocked down and replaced by high-rise flats.

Inner suburbs

Around the inner city are the **inner suburbs** [Figure 4]. This is a residential area of larger **semi-detached** houses with back gardens, built in the 1920s to 1950s. There is open space around the houses, such as parks, and some shopping parades.

▼ Figure 4: Lincoln's inner suburbs

Outer suburbs

Around the inner suburbs are the **outer suburbs** [Figure 5]. These are residential areas, with a mixture of large detached houses and modern housing estates. There are more parks and services that take up large areas, for example sports centres, golf courses and out-of-town shopping centres.

▼ Figure 5: Lincoln's outer suburbs

Urban-rural fringe

The **urban–rural fringe** [Figure 6] is the area of land immediately around the town. It may be an area of **green belt**, farmland or open space. Some larger towns and cities do not have much open space along their outer edges. Instead, they have continued to grow to join neighbouring settlements. This creates large continuous urban areas called **conurbations**.

▼ Figure 6: Lincoln's urban–rural fringe

What can you describe about each zone by looking at the photographs of Lincoln?

4·8 Cities in LEDCs

The world's major cities are growing rapidly, but since the 1950s cities in LEDCs have grown much faster than those in MEDCs. Many of these have populations over 10 million and are called **megacities**. Figure 1 shows the biggest megacities in 2003 and how they might change by 2015.

The land use in LEDC cities is different from MEDC cities (see pages 48–49).

In a typical LEDC city many of the wealthier inhabitants live in apartments or guarded **enclaves** near the city centre (or along a main road leading to the city centre). They have easy access to the CBD where shops, services, entertainment and offices are located.

▼ Figure 1: Megacities in 2003 and 2015 (estimate)
Figures are in millions

Top five megacities in 2003	Top five megacities in 2015
Tokyo 35	Tokyo 36
Mexico City 18.7	Mumbai 22.6
New York–Newark 18.3	Delhi 20.9
Sao Paulo 17.9	Mexico City 20.6
Mumbai 17.4	Sao Paulo 20

Figure 1 shows the top five megacities in 2003 and the predicted top five in 2015. How many of these megacities are in LEDCs and how many are in MEDCs?

▼ Figure 2: Land use in a typical LEDC city (Model first produced by Ford and Griffin, 1980)

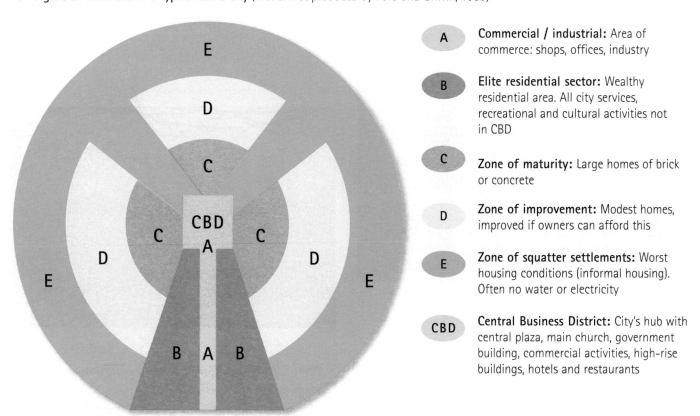

A — Commercial / industrial: Area of commerce: shops, offices, industry

B — Elite residential sector: Wealthy residential area. All city services, recreational and cultural activities not in CBD

C — Zone of maturity: Large homes of brick or concrete

D — Zone of improvement: Modest homes, improved if owners can afford this

E — Zone of squatter settlements: Worst housing conditions (informal housing). Often no water or electricity

CBD — Central Business District: City's hub with central plaza, main church, government building, commercial activities, high-rise buildings, hotels and restaurants

Squatter settlements

The poorer inhabitants will live in **squatter settlements**. Squatter settlements are commonly called shanty towns, but in Brazil they are called favelas, in India they are known as bustees, and in the Philippines they are called barong-barong. **Figure 3** shows a squatter settlement in Mumbai, India.

Squatter settlements are unplanned shelters or shacks built from cheap or scrap materials such as cardboard, wood and cloth. They are usually located on the edge of cities, or sometimes inside the cities on derelict land or near rubbish tips. The inhabitants do not own the land they build on. The land available is often steep or poorly drained. Most squatter settlements lack basic services, such as running water, electricity, and sanitation – and they are very crowded. As well as rubbish tips, there are usually open sewers which frequently overflow in heavy rain, running down the unsurfaced streets and spreading disease.

Making improvements

Whilst squatter settlements have many problems, many of the older ones are gradually being improved. Wood and scrap materials have been replaced by bricks. Running water, electricity and sanitation have been put in. Local clinics and schools have been built. In some areas local people are even raising money by organising tours for tourists!

▼ Figure 3: A squatter settlement (bustee) in Mumbai

Look at the photo of Mumbai [**Figure 3**]. What would it be like to live in high rise appartments compared to the squatter settlements?

4·9 City problems

Many people want to live in cities because of the services and jobs that they offer. As a result of their large populations however, all cities have problems – especially to do with transport.

Transport problems

The huge growth in car ownership over the last thirty years has changed how our cities look. In Britain in 1972, just over half (52 per cent) of households had access to at least one car. In 2002 this had risen to 73 per cent. There has also been a growth in the number of households having three or more cars or vans, from 2 per cent in 1972 to 6 per cent in 2002 [Figure 1].

People living near the CBD may use public transport or walk to get to work or the shops, but many **commuters** and people in the suburbs use cars. Cars offer door-to-door transport, so are very popular with those who can afford them.

It isn't only cars that cause problems in towns and cities. **Freight** used to be carried by canal and rail, but most is now carried by road.

▼ Figure 1: British households with access to a car or van (1972–2002)

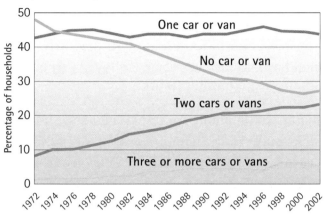

Between 1980 and 2002 the amount of road freight traffic in Britain increased by 67 per cent. Lorries damage road surfaces more than cars and their weight causes vibration damage to buildings.

> Look at **Figure 2**, which suggests some problems related to transport within a city. Can you think of any others?

▼ Figure 2: Transport problems in a city

Vibration damage to buildings

Air pollution

Visual pollution

Noise pollution

Traffic congestion

Accidents

Lack of parking spaces

Damage to roads

Key Words: commuters, freight see page 124

Transport solutions

Planners use two main ways to try to solve the problems caused by too many cars:

- slow down or reduce the amount of private transport
- improve public transport and make it a more attractive option.

Figure 3 shows some examples of solutions already being used in the UK.

Other city problems

Cities have many other types of problems apart from transport, for example overcrowding, litter, graffiti, crime and homelessness.

> Think of a typical problem found in a city (not transport). Explain the problem and what can be done to help solve it. It could be a problem happening in an area near you.

▼ Figure 3: Solving traffic problems

	Solutions
Reduce private transport	**Congestion charge**: for example Central London. The scheme began in April 2003. It cost £5 per day to drive in the zone. After six months, 50 000 fewer vehicles were entering the zone per day. By law, all the income must be spent on improving London's transport facilities.
	Reduce car numbers: for example London. Members of 'WhizzGo' can use a small car for up to £5.50 per hour. This covers all expenses except fines and damage. All cars are new energy-efficient models. Case studies show that for every club car at least five people will sell or scrap their existing cars.
Slow private transport	**Street calming**: for example West Ealing, London. Unhappy locals formed an action group and asked the local council to establish a Home Zone. Since 2002 they have introduced controlled parking and traffic calming measures (for example speed-bumps), closed a major 'rat-run', and put in better street lighting.
	Reduce speed limits: for example Hursley, Hampshire. Locals were angry at the traffic speeding through their village which had caused crashes. An action group was set up and complained to the council. The council conducted speed checks and reduced the speed limit to 30 mph.
Improve public transport	**Trams**: for example Midland Metro. An electric tram service opened from Wolverhampton to Birmingham in the summer of 1999. Where they run on the road they have priority over other traffic, so there are few delays. Nottingham also opened a new tram service in 2004.
	Park and Ride: for example Cambridge. Easy-access buses serve five car parks around the edge of the city. Buses run every 10 minutes during the day and 20 minutes after 7 pm. A day return costs only £1.80 with up to three children free.

4·10 Changing rural settlements in MEDCs

In MEDCs, many people who are looking for a better quality of life choose to move out of cities into the countryside. This is called **urban-rural migration** or counter-urbanisation. **Figure 1** shows that more people are migrating from urban to rural areas each year than the number migrating from rural to urban areas. In England, 14 million people now live in rural areas, 23 per cent of the population.

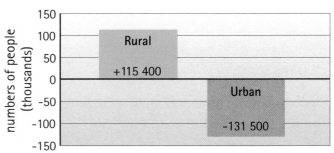

▼ Figure 1: Net migration in rural and urban England, June 2001–2002

What are the main reasons for people wanting to move from urban to rural areas?

Problems in rural areas

When people move from urban to rural areas it can have many effects. A rural settlement with a lot of commuters in its population is known as a **dormitory town**, as these people only return home during weekdays to sleep. As a result, they may not become involved in the life of their local community.

Some people don't want to commute long distances, yet like the peace of the countryside. They may buy a **second home** there to use at weekends and holidays. They often buy food in their own local supermarkets to take with them.

This means small village stores can suffer where there are many second homes. They may be forced to close – leaving permanent residents without local shops.

People from urban areas are used to paying higher house prices. This can force up the price of houses in rural areas. Ludlow is an attractive market town [**Figures 2a and 2b**] and has become a very popular area to move to. In 2003–2004, extra demand meant that house prices there increased by an average of 19 per cent. This makes it very difficult for local young adults to afford to buy houses. They are forced to move out of their local area, live with their parents, or even become homeless or 'sofa-surfers'. The proportion of homeless households in remote rural districts rose by almost 30 per cent in 2002–2004.

▼ Figure 2a: View of Ludlow, Shropshire

Key Words: urban–rural migration, dormitory town see page 124

▼ Figure 2b: View of Ludlow, Shropshire

As people move out, village services are lost – post offices, general stores, doctor's surgeries and primary schools close. Local people must travel further to reach services, yet bus services become less frequent or are cut completely. This leads to **rural deprivation**.

Sometimes there is conflict between newcomers and existing residents. However, if people work together the whole community can benefit. For example in Ditton Priors [Figures 3a and 3b], the locals are actively involved in their community. They support a wide range of shops and services (listed on page 42). The village hall has a computer room and is used for a range of activities including badminton, a senior citizen luncheon club, bowls and a nursery. The village is linked with Simplé, a village in northern France.

Unemployment in rural areas is also a problem. Machinery is used increasingly in farming, so there are fewer jobs. Many young adults, and particularly men, migrate to urban areas to look for jobs. They also look for more entertainment opportunities, such as cinemas and clubs. Other young people leave rural areas to go to college. As a result, many remote villages have increasingly elderly populations.

▼ Figures 3a and 3b: Views of Ditton Priors, Shropshire

Key Words: rural deprivation see page 124

4·11 Why do we need more new homes?

After World War II, areas of green belt were put around the larger cities in Britain. This was to stop urban areas from spreading out in an unplanned way into the countryside. It is difficult to get planning permission to build a new building or even extend an existing building in the green belt.

New Towns

At the same time, **New Towns** [Figure 1] like Bracknell in Berkshire [Figures 2a and 2b] were built outside the green belts. These were to provide homes for the **overspill population** from cities. They were needed because the population was growing rapidly. Many old inner city areas had either been destroyed in the war or were in a poor condition.

New Towns have a regular street pattern and a number of self-contained neighbourhoods with houses, shops and other local services. Modern industrial estates are located on the outskirts of

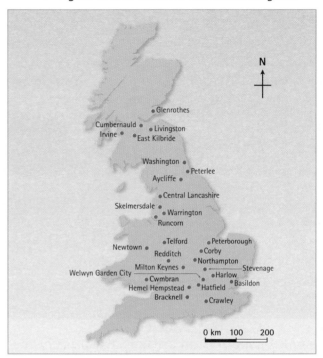

▼ Figure 1: New Towns in the United Kingdom

towns, where they are easily accessed by main roads and motorways. They are separated from areas of housing by public open spaces.

> Make a list of the push and pull factors which led to people moving to New Towns.

▼ Figures 2a and 2b: Views of Bracknell New Town

Modern terraced housing in Birch Hill

Bracknell's pedestrianised shopping centre

Key Words: New Towns see page 124

Housing shortages

New Towns were successful in providing many extra homes. However there is an increasing demand for new housing today. This is because the population is still growing and many more people are living alone. Many people are moving from the north of Britain towards Southeast England, where there are more job opportunities and better wages. This means that the worst housing shortages are in the Southeast.

The government estimate that more than 3.2 million new homes will be needed by 2016. Each region in the UK has been set a target for the number of new homes that must be built within a certain time. For example, 200 000 are to be built in four main areas of the Southeast [Figure 3].

The government has promised £930 million to spend on **infrastructure** and improved transport links for these areas.

Much of this new building will be on **greenfield sites**. These are rural areas or open spaces inside urban areas that have

▼ Figure 3: The four growth areas and existing areas of green belt around London

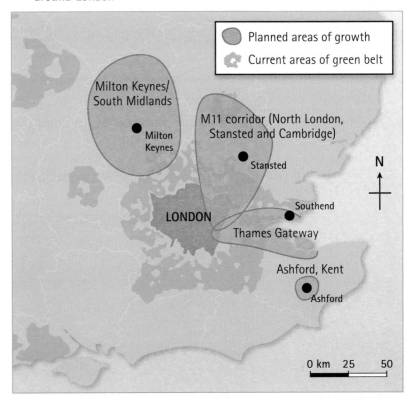

▼ Figure 4: A brownfield site

not been built on before. Building on these sites is often unpopular with local people who may complain to the local council to try to stop the new development. They are often known as **NIMBYs**.

New buildings can also be built on **brownfield sites**. These are areas that have been built on before, for example derelict sites in urban areas [Figure 4]. However, it can be more expensive as sometimes buildings have to be demolished first. The site may also be polluted by dangerous or toxic materials. The government wants 60 per cent of new homes to be on brownfield sites. To help they are offering grants to help pay for removing pollution.

Can you think of any greenfield or brownfield sites near where you live?

4·12 Building new homes

Investigation

You are a member of Redborough City council. The council has been asked to approve a site for a new housing estate with 200 dwellings. **Figure 1** shows the four possible sites for the development.

Figure 1: Four possible sites for a new housing estate of 200 dwellings near Redborough

A = the Lidd valley. An area of green belt

D = a brownfield site north of the village of Sawley

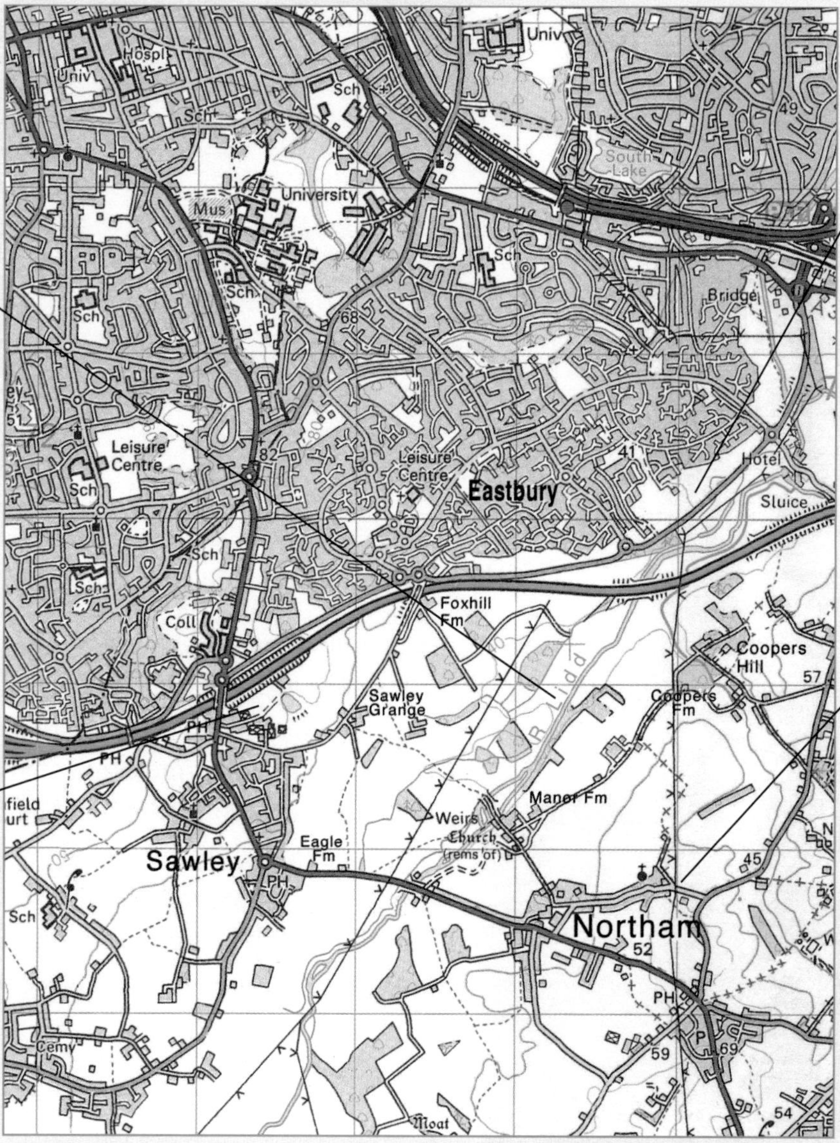

B = a greenfield site on the edge of Eastbury, an outer suburb of Redborough

C = a greenfield site in the village of Northam

Make a large copy of the table below.

- Using the information in **Figure 1** list the advantages and disadvantages of developing each site.
- From what you have read so far, which site do you think should be developed?

Site	Advantages	Disadvantages	Rank
A			
B			
C			
D			

Before you can make a decision about which site should be developed, you also need to consider how local people might be affected. The views of four locals are shown below:

Eastham resident:
We already have one of the biggest housing estates in Europe. There is so little open space that we don't want any more development here!

Northam Resident:
The village has grown very fast over the last few years and it is already losing the lovely quiet rural character that it had when I first moved here. I don't want it to become just another suburb of Redborough.

Environment Agency Officer:
The River Lidd has very good water quality with many fish and invertebrates living in it. The nearby woods have deer and many small mammals and birds living in them. Development will not be good for the wildlife.

Sawley Resident:
The site of the old nursery on the edge of the village is very ugly. There are huge greenhouses with every pane smashed. Anything would be an improvement.

- Use the opinions above to add to your list of advantages and disadvantages of each site.
- Rank the sites, giving 1 to the site that you believe most strongly that the council should allow to be developed and 4 to the site that you do not feel should be developed at any time.
- Has your answer changed?

5·1 The hydrological cycle

The hydrological (or water) cycle is one of the Earth's most important systems. A **system** is something which contains many different parts working together. If the system is a cycle, like the hydrological cycle, the parts work together, continuously, circulating round. **Figure 1** shows the six **processes** which move water around the system. It shows how these fit together within the system to make the hydrological cycle work.

The hydrological cycle can be divided into different parts called **inputs**, **stores**, and **outputs**. The main input is water or **precipitation** – any moisture which falls from the sky including rain, snow and sleet.

As precipitation falls, it starts its journey around the hydrological cycle, moving between stores. For example, rain can be stored on the Earth's surface in rivers, lakes and oceans, on plants, or frozen as ice or snow. It can be stored underground in the soil or in rocks.

> Can you think of any other important systems? They can be natural ones like the hydrological cycle, or ones made by people.

▼ Figure 1: The hydrological cycle

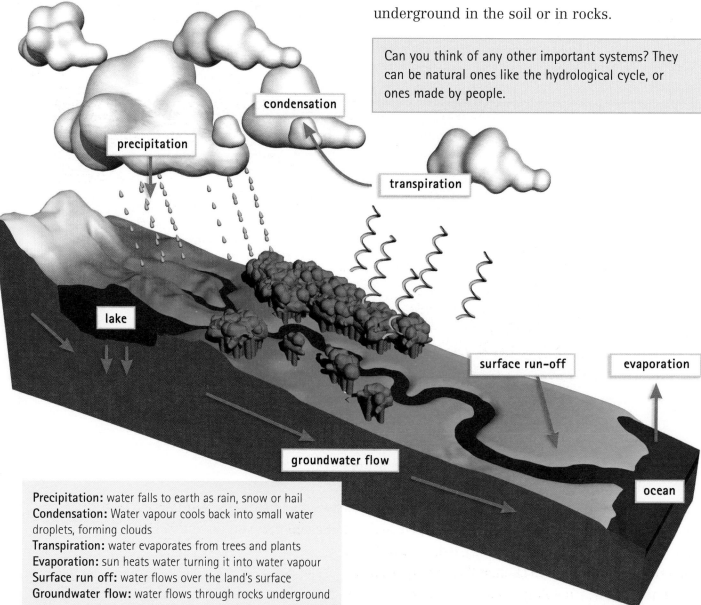

Precipitation: water falls to earth as rain, snow or hail
Condensation: Water vapour cools back into small water droplets, forming clouds
Transpiration: water evaporates from trees and plants
Evaporation: sun heats water turning it into water vapour
Surface run off: water flows over the land's surface
Groundwater flow: water flows through rocks underground

Key Words: **system, processes, inputs, stores, outputs, precipitation** see page 124

It can also be stored in the atmosphere – as tiny droplets of water in clouds or in the air as water vapour. The processes in Figure 1 show water in its various forms moving between these stores.

Rivers play a very important part in the hydrological cycle. They collect and store water from the surrounding area and also move it from the land to the seas and oceans. Each river drains an area of land called a **drainage basin** [Figure 2].

▼ Figure 2: A drainage basin

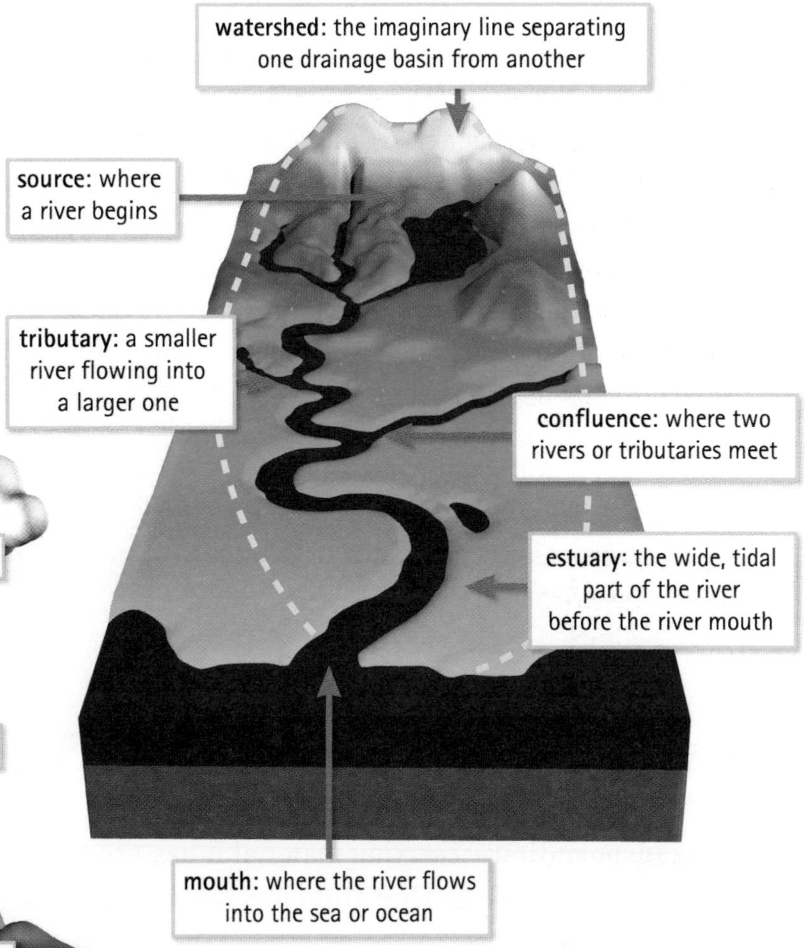

watershed: the imaginary line separating one drainage basin from another

source: where a river begins

tributary: a smaller river flowing into a larger one

confluence: where two rivers or tributaries meet

estuary: the wide, tidal part of the river before the river mouth

mouth: where the river flows into the sea or ocean

▼ Figure 3: How water moves through its drainage basin

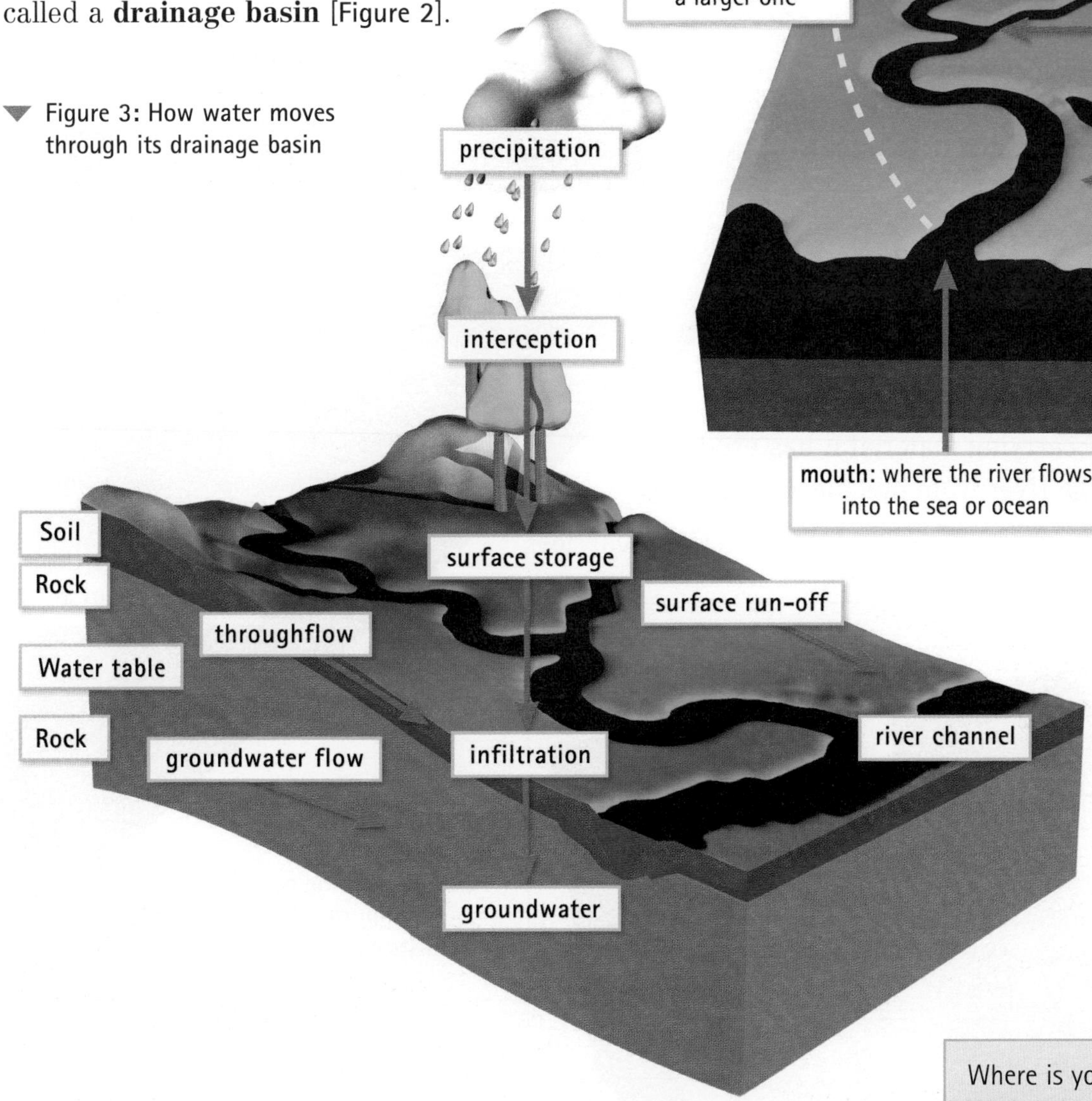

precipitation

interception

surface storage

surface run-off

Soil

Rock

throughflow

Water table

Rock

groundwater flow

infiltration

river channel

groundwater

Figure 3 shows in more detail what happens to water in a drainage basin. A drainage basin is really a small system itself, working inside the hydrological cycle. Just like the hydrological cycle, it has different processes helping to move water around between stores.

Where is your nearest river? What is it called? Find a suitable map (an OS map is best) and identify the river and its drainage basin.

5.2 How rivers work

Rivers are dynamic parts of the landscape – they are constantly moving and changing. Page 61 explained how they move water from the land to seas and oceans, but they do much more than that. Running water is very powerful; it shapes the land over which it flows. The more powerful and faster the flow of the water, the more energy it has. The more energy it has, the more it can change and shape the landscape in and around it.

Figures 1, 2, 3 and 4 show a river at work. Just like the hydrological cycle, different processes take place within a river. These processes are:

- **erosion** – wearing away the land, either by the water itself or by the material it carries, for example stones scraping away the land

- **transportation** – carrying material it has eroded or which falls into the river from one place to another

- **deposition** – dropping or depositing the material it carries.

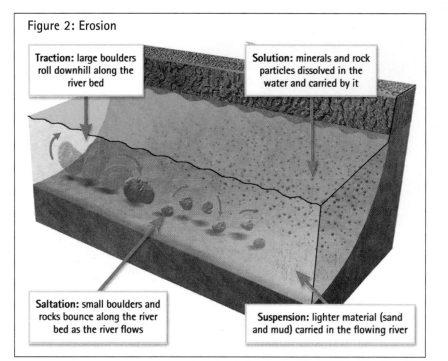

upper course

middle course

▲ Figure 1: The course of a river showing the three different parts of its course

Figure 2: Erosion

Traction: large boulders roll downhill along the river bed

Solution: minerals and rock particles dissolved in the water and carried by it

Saltation: small boulders and rocks bounce along the river bed as the river flows

Suspension: lighter material (sand and mud) carried in the flowing river

Key Words: erosion, transportation, deposition see page 124

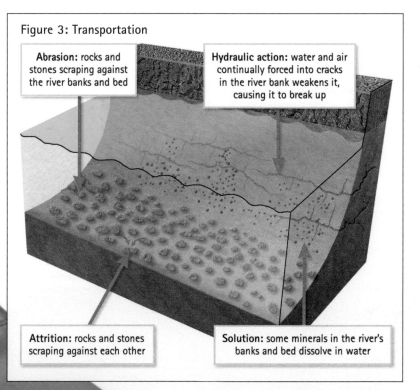

Figure 3: Transportation

Abrasion: rocks and stones scraping against the river banks and bed

Hydraulic action: water and air continually forced into cracks in the river bank weakens it, causing it to break up

Attrition: rocks and stones scraping against each other

Solution: some minerals in the river's banks and bed dissolve in water

Figure 1 shows the route or course taken by a river from its source in the mountains downhill to the sea. Geographers usually divide the course of the river into three sections: the **upper**, **middle** and **lower** courses. This is because in each section, different processes help to create different landforms.

Which process is **dominant** depends on the **gradient** (how steeply the land slopes), the size of the **river channel** (the width and depth of the river), and the **flow** (the speed of the water).

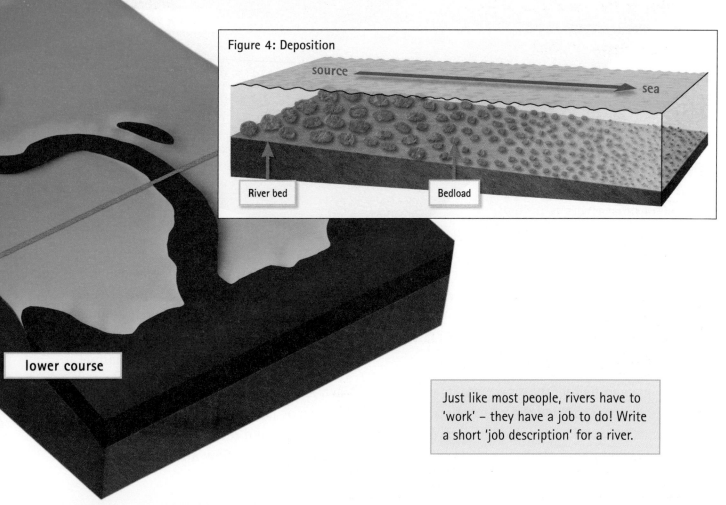

Figure 4: Deposition

source

sea

River bed

Bedload

lower course

Just like most people, rivers have to 'work' – they have a job to do! Write a short 'job description' for a river.

Rivers: the upper course

Figure 1: The upper course of a river

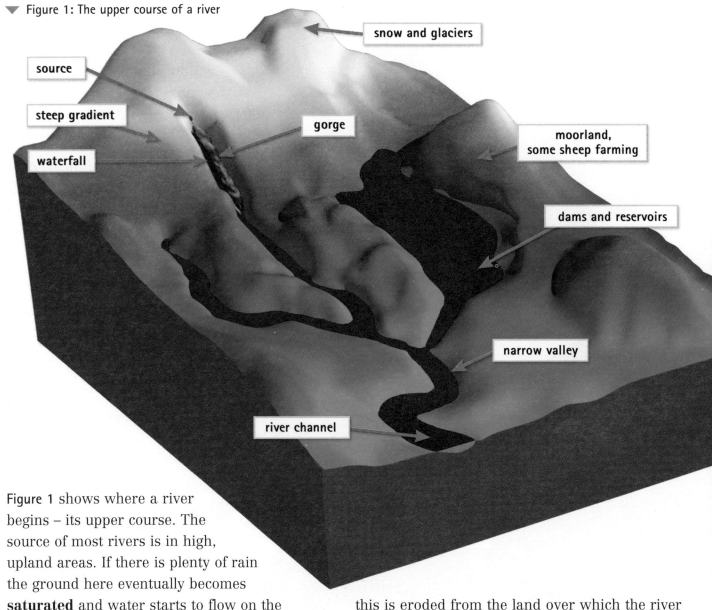

snow and glaciers

source

steep gradient

gorge

moorland, some sheep farming

waterfall

dams and reservoirs

narrow valley

river channel

Figure 1 shows where a river begins – its upper course. The source of most rivers is in high, upland areas. If there is plenty of rain the ground here eventually becomes **saturated** and water starts to flow on the surface. Alternatively if there is snow and ice, this will melt in warmer weather and flow downhill. Steep slopes help the water to flow quickly downhill.

At this stage in its life, the river uses its energy to erode downwards into the soil and rock – a process called **vertical erosion**. It starts to cut a narrow river channel. It also carries or transports a lot of material or **bedload**. Some of this is eroded from the land over which the river flows, other material may fall into it. Quite large pieces of rock can be transported by the river. These help it erode the land even more as they scrape or bounce along the river channel.

Each section or part of a river has distinctive features or landforms [Figure 2]. The type of landforms found mainly depend on the size and speed of the river flow and the type of rock it passes over.

Key Words: saturated, vertical erosion, bedload see page 124

▼ Figure 2: The characteristics of a river in its upper course

River channel	narrow, shallow
Flow	fast
Gradient	very steep
Valley	next to river channel, steep sided, narrow, v-shaped
Weather/climate	wet, cold
Erosion	mainly vertical erosion – cutting down into the land
Transportation	carries a wide range of material, from large rocks to fine sediment
Deposition	very little, some large rocks on river bed
Landforms/ features	source, rapids, waterfalls, gorges
Human activity landuse	moorland, sheep farming, dams and reservoirs
Settlement	very little, occasional farm

Waterfalls [Figure 3] are one of the most common features found in the upper course of rivers. Figure 4 shows you how they are formed.

▼ Figure 3: Waterfall

▼ Figure 4: How a waterfall forms

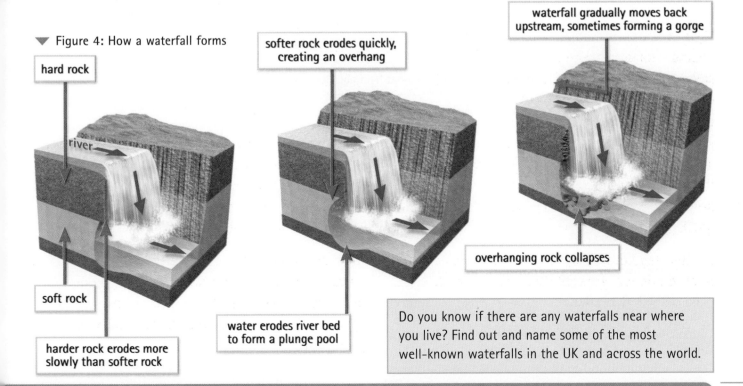

hard rock

river

soft rock

harder rock erodes more slowly than softer rock

softer rock erodes quickly, creating an overhang

water erodes river bed to form a plunge pool

waterfall gradually moves back upstream, sometimes forming a gorge

overhanging rock collapses

Do you know if there are any waterfalls near where you live? Find out and name some of the most well-known waterfalls in the UK and across the world.

5·4 Rivers: the middle course

Figure 1 shows some typical features of the middle course of a river. Rivers start to change in their middle course as they slow down, no longer flowing down steep slopes. The river channel becomes wider and deeper and the river starts to bend or **meander** across the valley floor or **flood plain**. The climate is usually warmer and drier than in the upper course, so more farming takes place. Cattle graze the rich grass on the flood plain and it is warm enough for crops to be grown on the flatter land.

▼ Figure 1: The middle course of a river

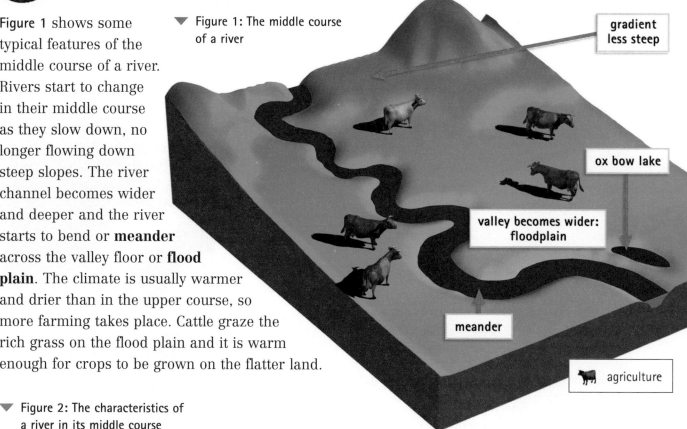

gradient less steep

ox bow lake

valley becomes wider: floodplain

meander

🐄 agriculture

▼ Figure 2: The characteristics of a river in its middle course

River channel	starts to become wider and deeper
Flow	slowing down
Gradient	less steep than in upper course, but still sloping
Valley	has become wider, with a flat floor and flood plain
Weather/climate	usually a little drier and warmer
Erosion	the river is still eroding downwards (vertical), but also outwards along the river banks and valley (lateral erosion)
Transportation	carrying lots of bedload, but the material is smaller and finer (attrition) or in solution
Deposition	as the river slows down it starts to deposit its bedload on the river bed and on the inside bends of meanders
Landforms/features	meanders, river cliffs, flood plain
Human activity/land use	farming – crops and livestock; industry
Settlement	farms, villages, small towns at bridging points

Now that the river is flowing more slowly, it begins to erode outwards or sideways – a process called **lateral erosion**. It also begins to deposit some of its bedload [Figure 2].

This helps form two distinctive features found in the middle course of a river – flood plains and meanders [Figure 3].

▼ Figure 3: The growth of a meander

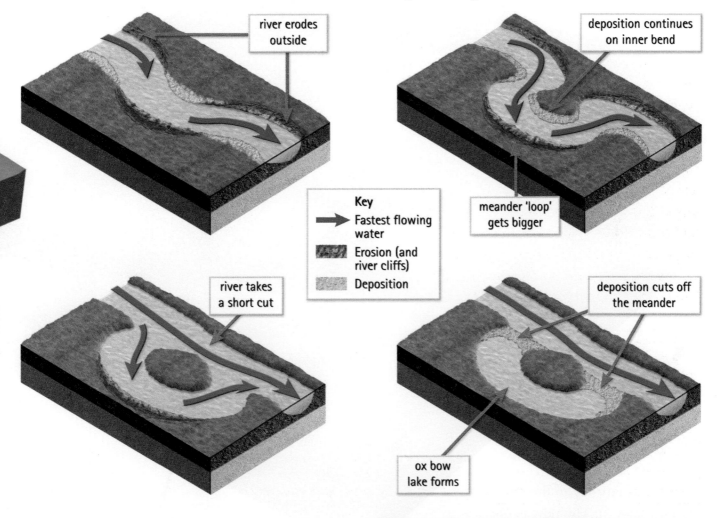

river erodes outside

deposition continues on inner bend

meander 'loop' gets bigger

Key
→ Fastest flowing water
▨ Erosion (and river cliffs)
░ Deposition

river takes a short cut

deposition cuts off the meander

ox bow lake forms

Many more settlements are found around the river and its valley along its middle course. Some developed as bridging points along the river. Others originally located near the river to be close to a water supply, or inside the bend of a meander to help defend the town from attack [Figure 4].

Describe the different processes at work as a meander develops. Why are meanders usually found in the middle course of a river, not in the upper course?

▼ Figure 4: An aerial view of Shrewsbury

Shrewsbury has developed on the inside of a meander – a good defensive position

Key Words: lateral erosion see page 124

Rivers: the lower course

▼ Figure 1: The lower course of a river

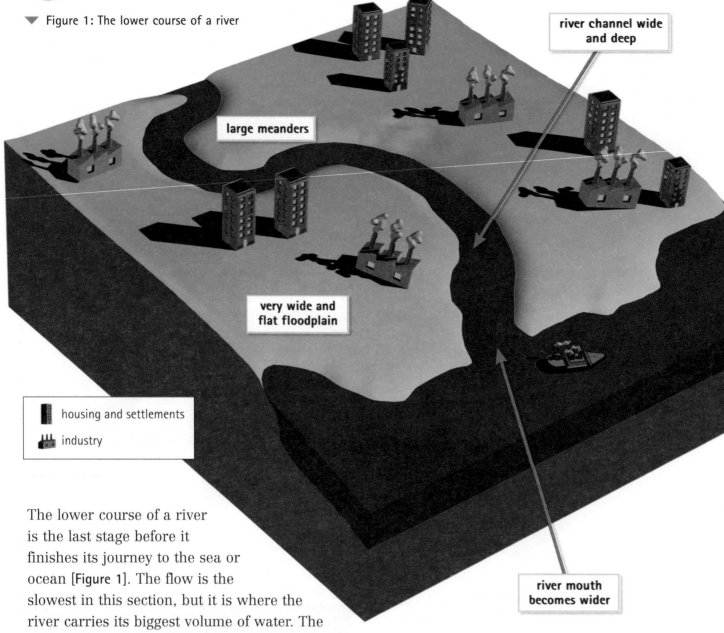

river channel wide and deep

large meanders

very wide and flat floodplain

housing and settlements

industry

river mouth becomes wider

The lower course of a river is the last stage before it finishes its journey to the sea or ocean [Figure 1]. The flow is the slowest in this section, but it is where the river carries its biggest volume of water. The river itself is at its widest and often its deepest here. It is also usually the part of the river where most human activity is found.

Quite complex processes take place where the river enters the sea or ocean at its mouth. Most rivers widen out into a **tidal** estuary. Here water flows out to sea and back into the river estuary twice a day. As it moves it deposits material over a large area. The mouth can become quite

shallow at low tide, revealing sand and mudflats. Over time, these **sediments** may become new layers of rock underwater.

Most of the distinctive landforms in this part of a river are the result of deposition because the river is flowing very slowly and transporting large amounts of sediment. Where artificial **embankments** or defences have not been built,

Key Words: tidal, sediments see page 124

natural embankments or **levees** are formed as rivers overflow onto the flood plain [**Figure 3**]. **Ox bow lakes** can also be found.

Some rivers enter the sea via spectacular landforms called **deltas**. This is where hundreds of tiny islands form, splitting up the river into smaller channels as the river drops tonnes of sediment. The River Nile [**Figure 4**] is one of the world's most famous deltas.

Rivers destroy rocks – and help make new ones. Explain why this statement is true.

▼ Figure 2: The characteristics of a river in its lower course

River channel	wide and deep, especially at the mouth
Flow	the slowest part of the river; but also tidal towards the mouth
Gradient	mainly flat
Valley	very wide and flat
Weather/climate	lowland, so warmer and drier than the upper course
Erosion	less than in other sections, but can increase during floods/high tidal flow
Transportation	carries lots of material suspended in solution or very fine grained sediment as bedload
Deposition	more deposition than in any other part of the river – embankments, flood plains, inside bends of meanders, mudflats in estuaries and mud/sand islands in deltas
landforms, features	embankments (levees), flood plain, meanders, ox bow lakes, estuary, delta, mouth
human activity/ land use	farming – crops and livestock, industry
settlement land use	large towns often with specialist functions, e.g. ports, seaside resorts, industrial centres

▼ Figure 3: The formation of river embankments

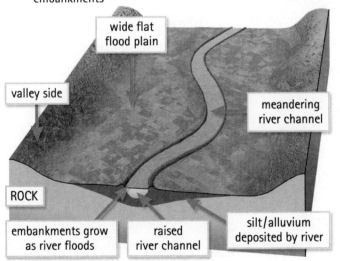

wide flat flood plain

valley side

meandering river channel

ROCK

embankments grow as river floods

raised river channel

silt/alluvium deposited by river

▼ Figure 4: The Nile Delta

The Nile Delta has hundreds of small islands built from material deposited by the river as it slows down before reaching the Mediterranean Sea

Key Words: embankments, levees, ox bow lakes, deltas see page 124

5·6 Rivers

▶ Investigation

Rivers on OS maps

You are going to identify some of the river features you have studied in this chapter. You will need to use the 1:25 000 OS map extract of the River Dovey (inside back cover). Part of this map is shown in **Figure 1**.

- Look at **Figure 1**. Make a list of any river features or landforms you can identify.
- Describe the river valley shown in **Figure 1**.

▼ Figure 1: Squares from OS map showing the River Dovey

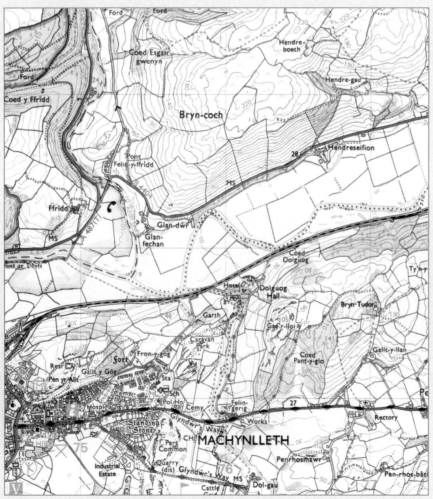

- Look at the whole map extract (inside back cover) and give six-figure grid references for:
  - a river confluence
  - a bridging point
  - a tributary of the River Dovey
  - a mountain stream.
- Describe the course of the River (Afon) Dulas.

UK Rivers

You are going to investigate a major river in Britain. Some of these are shown on **Figure 2**.

- Use an atlas to locate and name the rivers marked on **Figure 2**.

- Decide which river you are going to investigate. It could be the one nearest to where you live.

- Start your investigation by drawing up a fact file about your river to summarise the main information, for example length, route, main towns etc. You might want to present this as a table.

▼ Figure 2: The major rivers of Britain

N

0 km 100   200

- Draw a more detailed map of your chosen river from source to mouth. You may decide to draw a rough sketch map first, and then a more accurate map with a scale.
  - Try to divide your river into its three main sections (courses). Mark and label these on your map.
  - Add the location of the main towns.
  - Try to identify a range of river features or landforms in each section of your river. Your work from Investigation A should help you.
- Find some images of your river. Look in books or on the internet. If your river is local, take some photographs. Present these as display work, along with your fact file and map.

Resources:

You may want to use smaller scale maps (rather than those in an atlas) to help draw your map and locate/identify places and features. These could be regional maps and/or OS maps at different scales, especially 1:50 000. You would need to use several maps at this scale to cover the length of the river.

The Ordnance Survey web link is www.ordsvy.gov.uk

The world's water supply

▼ Figure 1: Availability of water per person by country in 2004

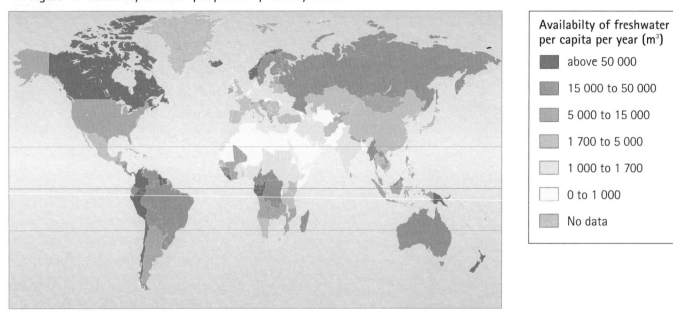

Availabilty of freshwater
per capita per year (m³)

- above 50 000
- 15 000 to 50 000
- 5 000 to 15 000
- 1 700 to 5 000
- 1 000 to 1 700
- 0 to 1 000
- No data

Water is an essential part of our daily lives. A clean, fresh water supply is a basic necessity for everyone – for good health, farming and industry. The demand for water continues to grow as the population increases and people expect a higher quality of life.

Of all the water in the world, only 2.5 per cent is freshwater. Only about 30 per cent of this freshwater is easily available for us to use [Figure 2b]. Yet the total amount of fresh water on earth could meet all our needs if it was evenly distributed and accessible. However, as Figure 1 shows, this is not the case. There are also major issues concerning the storage and pollution of water.

Do you ever think about where the water you use comes from, how you use it yourself and how it is used for you?

▼ Figure 2a: The world's fresh water availability

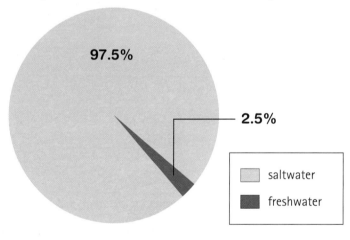

97.5%

2.5%

- saltwater
- freshwater

▼ Figure 2b: Sources of the world's fresh water

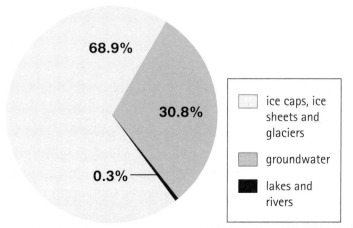

68.9%

30.8%

0.3%

- ice caps, ice sheets and glaciers
- groundwater
- lakes and rivers

The scale of the problem

- 25 per cent of the world's population struggle to obtain enough water now
- Total world water use is increasing at a rate of 2.5 per cent per year
- We use six times more water now than we did in 1900
- Many regions receive enough rainfall, but are unable to capture and store enough to use in times of drought [Figure 3]
- Two billion people lack access to safe water and three billion lack effective sanitation
- Dirty water in LEDCs causes 80 per cent of illnesses, killing 10 million people annually
- 70 per cent of all the water used by people is for agriculture. In many places, especially in MEDCs, farming activities have led to serious pollution of water supplies [Figure 4].

The problem is enormous and getting worse:

- By 2025 up to two-thirds of the world's population will lack sufficient water. Twenty-seven countries will face a severe water crisis
- By 2100 the availability of water in Africa will be reduced from 9000 to 1600 cubic metres per person
- Over 300 major river basins cross national boundaries. They are a potential cause of conflicts over access to water
- water shortages will cause a slow down in economic growth.

▼ Figure 3: Farmoor reservoir, Oxfordshire, UK

A multipurpose water scheme that manages water supply, recreation (boating and fishing) as well as nature conservation.

▼ Figure 4: Green algae on the surface of a drainage ditch in Oxfordshire, UK

Fertiliser washed into water from nearby fields can pollute water. It causes algae to grow and cover the surface. This blocks out sunlight, a process called eutrophication.

Providing clean water can be very expensive. Many communities and countries struggle to find enough money to improve their access to water and **sanitation**. Outside funding is sometimes used from international organisations and charities. For example, since 1950, the **World Bank** has lent over $36 billion for water development.

How would your life be different if you did not have enough clean water?

5·8 Access to water and sanitation

Access to a plentiful supply of clean water and good sanitation are important issues. Without them, it is difficult for countries to develop. In 1994, 34 per cent of the world's population lived in countries with significant water shortages.

By 2025 this is likely to rise to 63 per cent. The most severe shortages are expected to be mainly in LEDCs in Africa, Asia, South and Central America. **Figure 1** gives information for access to water and adequate sanitation in the year 2000.

▼ Figure 1: Global water supply and sanitation coverage, 2000 (Figures have been rounded to the nearest 100 million)

	World population (billions) total	with access	without access	% of world population with access	without access
Urban water supply	2.9	2.6	0.3	90	10
Rural water supply	3.2	2.3	0.9	71	29
Total water supply	6.1	4.9	1.2	80	20
Urban sanitation	2.9	2.5	0.4	86	14
Rural sanitation	3.2	1.2	2.0	38	62
Total sanitation	6.1	3.7	2.4	60	40

Why do you think figures for water supply and sanitation in urban and rural areas are given separately? Can you see any major differences?

Water Supply

12 500 cubic kilometres (km^3) of water are available for human use per year. The amount actually used for all purposes today is approximately 3 700 cubic kilometres per year. If all the available water were shared out evenly each person would have 6 600 cubic metres per year. As demand increases, the amount available is predicted to fall to 4 800 cubic metres per person by 2025. By 2025, up to 3 billion people may be living in countries with less than 1 700 cubic metres of water per person per year.

The world's available freshwater supply is unevenly distributed. It also varies seasonally, and from year to year. In many LEDCs, freshwater comes from seasonal monsoon rains. These can be unreliable and unpredictable, and their failure to arrive can lead to sudden water shortages.

▼ Figure 2: Bottled water

It's expensive to be poor

In Port-au-Prince, Haiti, a survey showed that households connected to the water system typically paid around $1.00 per cubic metre. Unconnected customers, who had to buy water from sellers, paid from $5.50 up to a staggering $16.50 per cubic metre.

In Lima, Peru, poor families on the edge of the city pay vendors roughly $3.00 per cubic metre, twenty times the price for families connected to the city system.

Bottled water is the most expensive form of water. In MEDCs we take it for granted but in LEDCs the poor cannot afford it.

In 2000, the United Nations Secretary General Kofi Annan said:

'No single measure would do more to reduce disease and save lives than bringing safe water and adequate sanitation to all.'

When little water is available, it has to be used for a wide range of purposes. It can quickly become dirty, polluted and unhealthy. In some places, like the Caribbean Island of St Lucia [**Figure 4**], women still use rivers for washing clothes. These same rivers are used for recreation and for cattle to drink from.

▼ Figure 4: Using a local river in St Lucia

Available water is often used for many purposes, by people and animals, and quickly becomes polluted

▼ Figure 3: Open sewers in St Lucia

Filthy, polluted water can easily spread disease, especially when it overflows into nearby homes

Too many people in LEDCs still lack access to water that is clean, safe and affordable. They often have little alternative but to buy expensive, bottled water from street vendors [**Figure 2**]. Many have inadequate sanitation, with open sewers or polluted streams running through settlements [**Figure 3**]. These are a major health hazard, especially in the wet season when they overflow and flood homes.

What evidence can you find to support the statement made by Kofi Annan?

Water consumption 1

The map on page 72 shows that the distribution of water resources across the world is uneven. So too is the amount of water we consume. A quarter of the world's population struggle to obtain enough water.

The following figures show how overall water use (measured in the amount of litres used per person per day) varies geographically:

- North America   400 litres
- Europe   200 litres
- Asia and Latin America   200–600 litres
- Sub-Saharan Africa   10–20 litres

Some areas use far more water than others. The highest figures are found in MEDCs and in countries where industry is growing quickly. In contrast, water use in Sub-Saharan Africa is dangerously low. The amount of water that is lost is a serious cause for concern. For example, in parts of Asia and Latin America up to 70 per cent is lost through leaks.

> Why do you think the amount of water people use varies so much from region to region?

▼ Figure 1: Global water consumption – use by sector

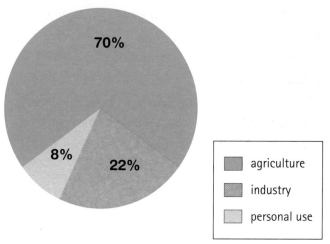

70%

8%

22%

- agriculture
- industry
- personal use

Water use: Agriculture

We use water in three main ways [Figure 1]. By far the biggest use is in agriculture (farming). Most of this is for **irrigation** – artificially watering crops. By using irrigation, farmers can grow crops on land that would be too dry for them to grow naturally. Many subsistence farmers in LEDCs live in arid regions, close to deserts. Egypt is mainly desert and has used water from the River Nile to irrigate farmland for thousands of years.

Irrigation is also used to add to natural water supplies in time of shortage – for example, around the Mediterranean where summers are hot and dry. In many MEDCs expensive irrigation schemes are often used to grow crops in arid regions and to produce high yields. A good example of this is the growing of salad crops in desert areas of Arizona and California in the southwest of the USA.

Farmers also need and use water for their livestock. In arid regions, boreholes are often dug to provide drinking water. As cattle are brought from the surrounding area, vegetation around the borehole can be trampled and over-grazed [Figure 2]. This can cause soil erosion and may even lead to **desertification** (see pages 88-89).

▼ Figure 2: Cattle and donkeys at a borehole, Owambo, Namibia

Key Words: desertification see page 124

Types of Irrigation

There are three main irrigation methods – flood, sprinkler and drip.

▼ Figure 3: Flood irrigation, Mariental, Namibia

Water is released from a main irrigation ditch. It gradually floods the crop in this gently sloping field

Flood irrigation:

uses the largest amount of water. Water is released from a drainage ditch to flood whole fields [Figure 3]. Sometimes underground pipes collect the water so it can be used again, but much water is lost through evaporation. The soil can also become very salty (salinisation). The land needs to slope for the water to spread without the need for pumps.

▼ Figure 4: Sprinkler or boom irrigation

Large sprinkler booms are wheeled into place by tractor to irrigate crops

Sprinkler or boom irrigation:

uses less water than flood irrigation. Large booms carrying sprinkler systems are wheeled into place [Figure 4]. These can be moved from field to field as required, irrigating large areas of crops.

▼ Figure 5: Drip or trickle irrigation

An efficient way of irrigating individual plants

Drip or trickle irrigation:

uses the least water. It is a system of pipes or hoses attached to small valves [Figure 5]. Each valve can be turned on, allowing a constant trickle of water to individual plants. It is an efficient way of watering small trees or large, individual plants. This system can also be used to bring fertilisers and pesticides to each individual plant as needed.

> What are the advantages and disadvantages of each type of irrigation?

Key Words: irrigation see page 124

5·10 Water consumption 2

Seventy per cent of the world's total water consumption is for farming (pages 76-77). The rest is used by industry or at home for personal use.

Water use: industry

Almost a quarter of water used is for industry. Factories use vast amounts of water to manufacture different goods – from cars to clothes. Increasingly, more and more water is being used in tourism, the world's fastest growing industry. New hotels and holiday complexes use large quantities of water [Figure 1]. Many have been built in arid areas, where tourists are attracted by a hot, dry climate. There is a growing concern that water use, especially in these regions, is **unsustainable**. This means that water is being used up at a faster rate than it can be replaced.

> Make a list of all the water demands a tourist might have.

Water use: personal use

Less than 10 per cent of water we use across the world is for personal or domestic use. This includes water used for washing, cleaning, cooking and sanitation. Although the average use is about 50 litres per person per day, the actual amount used varies greatly across the world. **Figure 2** shows the average amount of water required for a range of different uses in the UK. In many LEDCs the total daily figure is less than 10 litres per day – about the same as we use to flush a toilet once.

▼ Figure 1: Swimming pool, Sedona, Arizona, USA

Water use like this in an arid region is unsustainable

▼ Figure 2: Household water use

Household water use	Amount used
Water for drinking and cooking	70 litres (average per person per week)
Washing machine	65 litres
Dishwasher	25 litres
Baths	80 litres
Shower	35 litres per normal shower (90 litres per power shower)
Toilet	7.5 litres per flush (9.5 litres pre-1993 toilets)
Hosepipe (in the garden or washing the car)	270 litres per half hour

Key Words: **unsustainable** see page 124

▼ Figure 3: Watering the garden

Using a sprinkler in the garden uses less than a hosepipe - but it still uses over 500 litres per hour!

How much water do you use in a day? In a week?

The future

In the UK today, each person uses an average of 150 litres of water a day. This is 70 per cent more than 30 years ago. Experts predict that with climate change, summers in the UK will become hotter and drier. This is when demands for water are already at their highest, so in future, water shortages could become more common. However, **Figure 4** shows that are a number of simple ways to reduce the amount we use and waste.

▼ Figure 5: Water butt collects rainwater for watering garden/ greenhouse plants

▼ Figure 4: Some ways to save water

SAVE WATER

- Don't leave taps running unnecessarily. A running tap wastes 5-10 litres of water a minute

- Take a shower, not a bath. It uses just about a third of the amount of water

- Install a low water use toilet flush. Standard flushes account for a third of water use in the home

- Fix dripping taps and leaks

- Only use a washing machine or dishwasher when there is a full load

- Save water (and energy) by using the minimum amount of water possible when boiling a kettle

- Wash the car with a bucket and sponge rather than a hosepipe. A hosepipe pipe can use up to 540 lites of water an hour!

- Collect rainwater in a container like the one shown to water plants and shrubs

Think about how you and your family – or your school – could use and waste less water.

Clean water

In the UK, we turn on the tap and expect unlimited, clean water. We pay water companies to provide clean water, and to remove, treat and clean our waste water. However, a third of the world's population, mainly those in LEDCs, do not have access to a safe and reliable water supply.

▼ Figure 1: Clean water

A resource that most people in the UK take for granted

Diseases

Many people have no alternative but to use dirty water. This doesn't just affect water for drinking, cooking and washing, but also water used for animals and crops. 80 per cent of the world's diseases are caused or spread by contaminated water [Figure 2]. Many of these are preventable by ensuring that the water is clean, but many are also easily treatable. Unfortunately, in countries with many water-borne diseases, people often lack adequate health care.

▼ Figure 2: Common water-borne diseases

Disease	Description
Cholera	Bacteria are spread by contaminated water/food. The main symptom is severe diarrhoea. Can kill in twenty-four hours.
Bacterial dysentery	Bacteria enter the body through water/food. Often carried by flies. Symptoms are fever and blood-stained diarrhoea. 140 million people affected, and 300 000 die each year.
Typhoid	Caused by drinking contaminated water. Symptoms are nausea, fever and diarrhoea. 17 million people affected each year, causing 600 000 deaths.
Bilharzia	Caused by flatworms resulting in chronic diarrhoea. Damage done to bladder, liver, kidneys. 200 million affected each year and 20 000 deaths.
Guinea worm	Parasitic worm enters body via contaminated water. Causes ulcers and fever. Worm eventually emerges through skin. Can grow to 1 metre in length.
Hookworm	Larvae of these parasitic worms are common in dirty latrines and enter body via soles of feet. Causes anaemia and stunted growth in children. The worm lives in the intestine and sucks blood.
Trachoma	Caused by bacteria, this is the main cause of preventable blindness. Causes sore, swollen eyelids. 4 million affected, mostly in areas where there is not enough water to wash regularly.

Globally, each year children under five suffer 1.5 billion episodes of diarrhoea, 4 million of which are fatal

> Try to find out about some of the treatments and cures for the diseases listed in Figure 2.

The clean water lottery

Every day in Mlakala, a village in the Machinga district of Malawi, the women collect the water their families need for cooking, washing and drinking. In this part of the world, the availability of clean drinking water is a lottery. Some days you win, some you lose – risking your health, even your life.

Most of the water that the women collect is from open pools. These are called **unprotected wells** because there is little to prevent contamination. When these are first dug, the soil acts as a natural filter, so the water is safe to drink. However, soon the rain washes in animal and human waste from surrounding fields. It pollutes the water with highly infectious micro-organisms. Several days later, people start to get ill with diarrhoea, constipation or dysentery. Boiling the water makes it safer, but there aren't many trees left to provide wood for a fire to heat it.

▼ Figure 3: Women and children in Malawi collecting water

▼ Figure 4: An open pool

Dozens of women and children trudge to Mlakala's well up to ten times a day. Unwashed hands and feet and dirty buckets help spread contamination to the well. In some villages more than a third of the children have been treated for water-borne illnesses, but far more suffer than receive treatment.

Malawi is one of the poorest countries in the world. A third of its people do not have proper food. The average **life expectancy** is just forty-four years. Water and sanitation are very poor. Over two-thirds of households use pit latrines. **Potable water** is available to only half the population.

> What could be done to stop the water becoming polluted, or to provide clean water?

Key Words: life expectancy, potable water see page 124

5·12 Flooding

Floods are one of the most common environmental hazards. In an 'average' year, floods account for:

- about a third of natural disasters
- more than half the deaths caused by natural disasters
- about a third of the economic losses due to natural disasters.

'At risk' environments

The most vulnerable environments are:

- low-lying flood plains and river estuaries. In Bangladesh floods caused by monsoon rains regularly cover 20 per cent of the flat land of the delta
- small river basins which suffer from **flash floods**
- low-lying coastal areas
- areas with steep slopes and high, intense rainfall
- areas downstream from inadequate dams.

In most MEDCs, deaths from floods are declining. The death rate in LEDCs is much greater, partly because warning systems and evacuation plans are poor. This is likely to increase as more people in LEDCs settle in low-lying areas.

Causes of floods

A flood occurs when a river is unable to contain all the water within its channel. As a result some spills over onto a flood plain. Floods can be the result of physical causes or human causes – or a mixture of the two [Figure 1].

▼ Figure 1: The causes of flooding

Physical causes

Heavy or sudden rain

Melting snow and ice

Storm surges on coast

Earthquakes/tsunamis

Landslides

Dam failure

Human causes

Climate change e.g. global warming

Urbanisation

Building on flood plains

Bridges and dams

River engineering e.g. embankments

Removal of plants and trees

Most floods in the UK occur when deep **depressions** (low pressure systems) bring heavy rain in autumn and winter. By contrast, in India, up to 70 per cent of the annual rainfall occurs in the summer monsoon. Elsewhere, melting snow is often the cause.

Find out about an area near your home where flooding has taken place.

▼ Figure 2: A flooded carpark

Too much water causes drains to overflow and flood

The growth of urban areas has worsened flooding by:

* creating **impermeable** surfaces that water cannot soak into, for example roads [**Figure 2**]
* channelling water quickly into nearby rivers through the network of drains, gutters and pipes

* Narrowing river channels and reducing the water they can carry, for example bridge supports across rivers
* Building on flood plains, taking away areas where rivers could flood safely and where water could soak into the ground.

Flood protection

Floods can be controlled by decreasing **runoff.** This can be done by:

* replanting areas of sparse vegetation or bare soil
* **contour ploughing** or building terraces
* protecting vegetation from fires, overgrazing and **deforestation**
* constructing small dams to trap water and sediment.

▼ Figure 3: Port Meadow, Oxford, during a flood

Why might building houses on a flood plain like this cause problems?

Have any new buildings (houses or factories) been built recently on a flood plain in your area? Have any been flooded?

5·13 Flooding in London

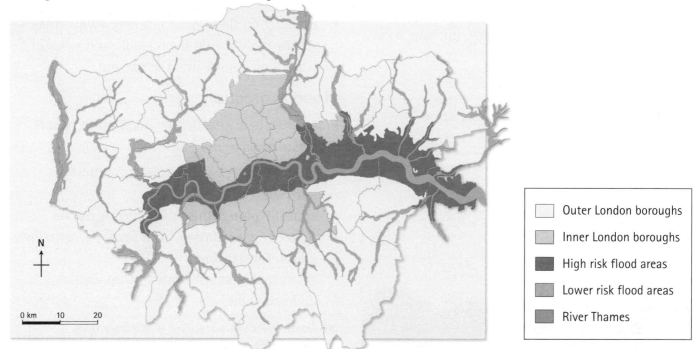

☐	Outer London boroughs
☐	Inner London boroughs
■	High risk flood areas
■	Lower risk flood areas
■	River Thames

Figure 1 shows the London boroughs, the River Thames and its tributaries. Half a million homes, 400 schools, 38 underground stations, 16 hospitals and 8 power stations are at risk from flooding. This risk is increasing because:

- Climate change is likely to cause the sea level to rise, higher tides and heavier winter rainfall in the UK. The Thames is tidal as far west as Teddington Lock, a stretch over 100 km long

- The southeast of England is gradually sinking. London is already a third of a metre lower (relative to sea level) than it was in 1945

- London needs to house over 700 000 extra people by 2016. A shortage of land has meant that thousands of homes have been built on flood plains. Many of the smaller tributaries of the River Thames have also been built over or **culverted**. Flood plains and tributaries would naturally soak up and contain flood water

- London has a combined sewer system that takes dirty, wastewater *and* surface runoff Much of it was built over 150 years ago, and some parts cannot cope with periods of sudden or very heavy rainfall.

▼ Figure 2: A main underground sewer in London

Many of London's sewers are over 150 years old and cannot cope with extreme or sudden heavy rainfall

Managing flood risks

Flooding is a natural process. It is almost impossible to stop it, so instead we try to plan to minimise the risk and damage. In 1983, the Thames Barrier [Figure 3] was opened. Its ten massive gates, separated by concrete piers, stretch 520 metres across the river at Woolwich. When very high tides are predicted, the ten gates can be lowered, protecting areas west of the barrier.

It was designed to cope with possible future floods until 2030. In the 1980s the gates were closed about once a year. In the 1990s this had increased to an average of four times a year. In 2003 alone it was closed eighteen times. Plans are already underway to upgrade the Barrier and associated defences at a currently estimated cost of £4 billion.

> Why is the risk of flooding in London likely to increase in the future? What can be done to lessen the risk?

▼ Figure 3: The Thames Barrier
Since it opened in 1983 it has had to be closed on average three times a year. However, in 2001 it closed 15 times.

The Thames Barrier is a major regional flood control scheme. However, at a more local level there are a number of measures which can be taken to reduce the risks of flooding in urban areas. These include not allowing new buildings on flood plains. Possible flood damage in new houses can be reduced by:

- Building solid concrete floors on the ground area
- Placing electrical sockets one metre or more above floor level
- Replacing chipboard/MDF kitchen units with PVC units (higher flood resistance)
- Installing temporary barriers at gates, doors and windows
- Using plaster with a higher flood resistance e.g. lime-based plaster
- Waterproofing external walls
- Installing one-way flap valves in drains to prevent back-up.

> Investigate your home. What could you do to help decrease damage from a possible flood?

5.14 Flooding in Bangladesh

Bangladesh is a country that suffers from flooding more than most. Floods occur every year between May and September.

Over 70 per cent of Bangladesh is flat, low-lying land less than 5 metres above sea level. Much of it forms the flood plain and delta around three major rivers – the Brahmaputra, Ganges and Meghna [Figure 1].

The weather also plays a major role. In May every year the **monsoon** arrives, bringing heavy rain for up to five months. Millions of tons of silt have made the river channels much shallower and more likely to flood. But the silt makes the land very fertile. **Tropical cyclones** are also common, sweeping in from the Bay of Bengal and bringing coastal and river flooding.

Bangladesh is a very crowded country with a rapidly increasing population. Land is scarce, and more and more homes are being built on flood plains. To the north, where the rivers begin, large areas of forest have been cut down to provide firewood. This has increased the speed at which rainfall and runoff reaches the rivers, increasing the flood risk.

List the physical and human factors which make Bangladesh at such a high risk from flooding.

▼ Figure 1: Satellite image of Bangladesh, showing the 3 main rivers and delta

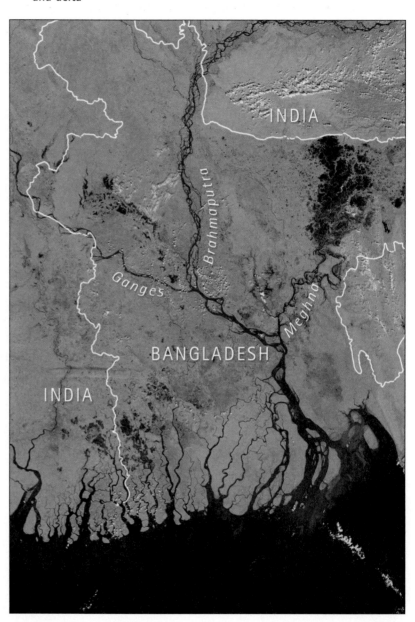

Effects of flooding

The annual floods (called **barsha**) cover up to 20 per cent of the country. Every five years or so flooding can be much worse. **Figure 4** shows that since 1950 there have been ten such major floods (called **bonna**). These can cover 40–60 per cent of the land. Such a flood happened in 2004.

2004 floods

Heavy rain from mid July to early September 2004 brought the worst flooding for ten years, covering 60 per cent of Bangladesh. 760 people died and 30 million people (over 20 per cent of the population) were displaced or made homeless. Many people fled to already overcrowded towns in search of food, shelter and work.

Tens of thousands suffered from water-borne infections and diseases. Twenty million people relied on food aid for up to a year after the floods, which destroyed the rice crop, food stores and killed livestock. The floods caused an estimated £7 billion worth of damage.

▼ Figure 2: Flooding in Dhaka, 2004

Managing flooding

With so much low-lying land, flooding will continue to be a problem for Bangladesh. To protect everyone adequately from flooding would take huge amounts of money. Bangladesh is an **LEDC** – it has not got the funds to spend on expensive flood control schemes. Much of the work taking place is on a local level and aimed at reducing the impact of floods, including:

- Constructing buildings on stilts
- Raising the height of river embankments
- Deepening river channels and building small dams
- Developing local flood warning system networks
- Building flood shelters and food stores

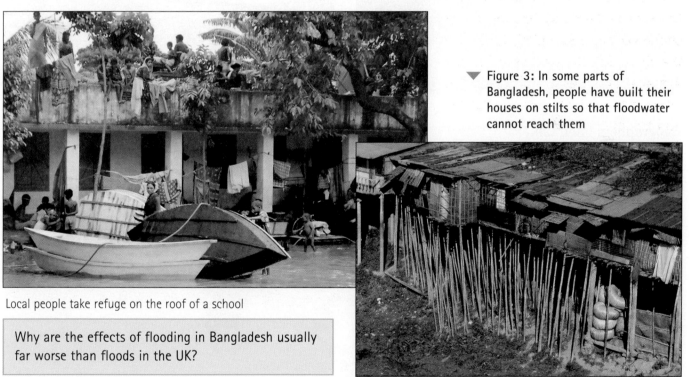

▼ Figure 3: In some parts of Bangladesh, people have built their houses on stilts so that floodwater cannot reach them

Local people take refuge on the roof of a school

Why are the effects of flooding in Bangladesh usually far worse than floods in the UK?

▼ Figure 4: Major floods in Bangladesh since 1950

1950   1955   1960   1965   1970   1975   1980   1985   1990   1995   2000   2005

5·15 The world's arid lands

About a third of the world's land experiences **arid** (dry) conditions. Whilst many arid regions are very hot [Figure 1], others like Antarctica [Figure 2] are very cold. True arid areas have less than 250mm of precipitation per year. **Semi-arid** places have between 250-500mm. Figure 3 shows where these are found.

▼ Figure 2: Cold desert – Antarctica

▼ Figure 1: Hot desert – Wadi Rum, Jordan

Geographers often talk about **water balance**. This is the input of water minus the output or 'loss' of water. Arid areas have a **negative water balance**. They lose more water, usually through evaporation, than they receive through precipitation. The Sahara Desert in Africa loses 200 times more water than it receives each year.

▼ Figure 3: The world's driest regions

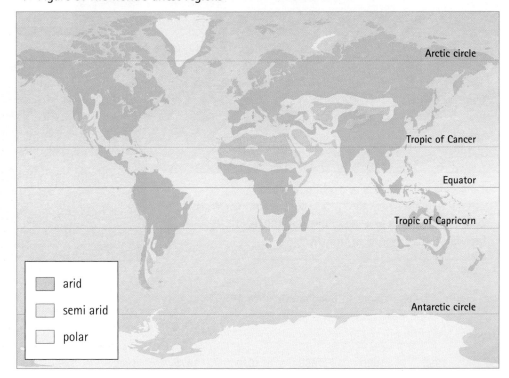

- arid
- semi arid
- polar

Arctic circle

Tropic of Cancer

Equator

Tropic of Capricorn

Antarctic circle

Living on arid lands

Despite the often harsh conditions, 650 million people live in the world's dry regions. Most of these live on the edges of deserts where there is some rainfall. Land use is very limited when there is no water and temperatures are very extreme. In these places, water is usually taken from the rocks deep underground. Rocks that can store water are called **aquifers** [Figure 4].

▼ Figure 4: An aquifer

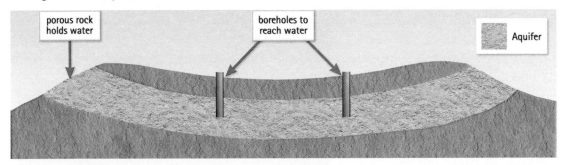

Aquifers supply water for irrigation. This makes it possible to farm in arid regions. With water, plants can grow and soils can develop.
In semi-arid areas, cattle or sheep ranching is possible without irrigation providing there is some access to drinking water.

Sometimes, areas on the edges of dry or desert regions can be overused. Too many cattle can destroy what little vegetation there is. This can leave the soil bare and worthless. It causes desert areas to start to spread, a process called **desertification**.

Tourism in arid areas

In other arid regions, such as Tunisia, Jordan and Dubai, guaranteed hot, dry weather is attractive to tourists [**Figure 5**]. Arid and semi-arid climates are also popular areas for building retirement homes and complexes, complete with swimming pools and golf courses. A good example is the Sun Belt region of the southwest USA. However, such developments use vast quantities of water. This is difficult and expensive to provide, especially in a sustainable way.

▼ Figure 5: A hotel complex

Tourists are attracted to hot, dry locations where providing enough water can be a major problem

Think about all the different ways water would be needed in a location like the one shown in **Figure 5**.

Key Words: aquifers, desertification see page 124

5·16 The Euphrates – a transnational river

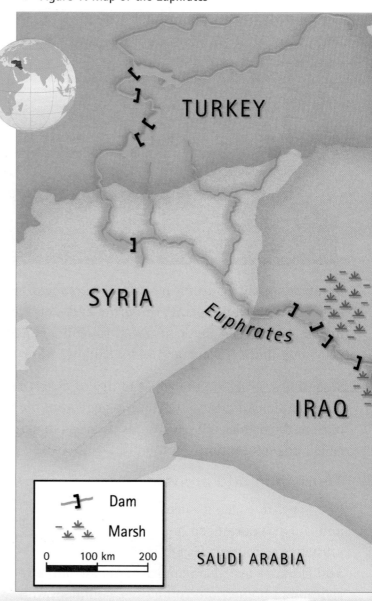

The world's largest rivers often cross several countries and act as the border between others. 'Transnational' rivers are often the cause of conflict. The Euphrates [**Figure 1**] meanders through ancient history (it is named in the Old Testament) and troubled modern politics.

Turkey

In the 1960s, Turkey began building a series of dams to generate electricity and increase farmland as part of the southeastern Anatolia project (GAP). Before the Ataturk Dam was completed in 1990, 30 km^3 of water passed along the Euphrates each year. It is now just 16 km^3 a year – and a cause of conflict with neighbouring Syria.

Syria

As Turkey began work on its dams, Syria was developing its own plans to use the Euphrates for irrigation and electricity. The Thawra Dam at Tabaqa created an artificial lake 80 km long, holding 12 billion cubic metres of water [**Figure 2**].

Whilst Syria has complained about Turkey's use of the Euphrates, it has stopped water from the Orantes, a smaller river in Syria, from flowing into Turkey.

▼ Figure 2: The Thawra Dam, Syria

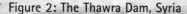

Iraq

The Thawra Dam in Syria, completed in 1973, reduced the amount of water from the Euphrates reaching Iraq. As a result, in 1974 Baghdad threatened to bomb the dam and even moved troops to the border. The quality of the water that does reach Iraq from the Euphrates is relatively poor and despite irrigation, crop yields are low. This is a real problem as Iraq has had to import up to 90 per cent of its food.

In 1998 Syria and Iraq agreed to work together against Turkey's activities on the Euphrates and its main tributary, the Tigris. This led to a boycott of companies involved in Turkey's GAP project.

The Tigris and Euphrates meet in Iraq 70 km north of Basra, creating a 20 000 km^2 wetland region, once home to 250 000 Marsh Arabs [Figure 3]. Only 40 000 live there today, partly because the marshes were drained as a way of punishing the people for their opposition to Saddam Hussain. The reduced flow in the Euphrates now means that it will never be possible to restore these wetlands in the south.

The Gulf

The Tigris and Euphrates together form the Shatt al-Arab waterway, part of the border between Iraq and Iran. Without the marshes to act as a natural filter to remove fertilisers, nutrient-rich water can pass straight into the sea. This encourages **algae blooms** or red tides which use up oxygen in the seawater. In 1999, one red tide killed 400 to 500 tonnes of fish.

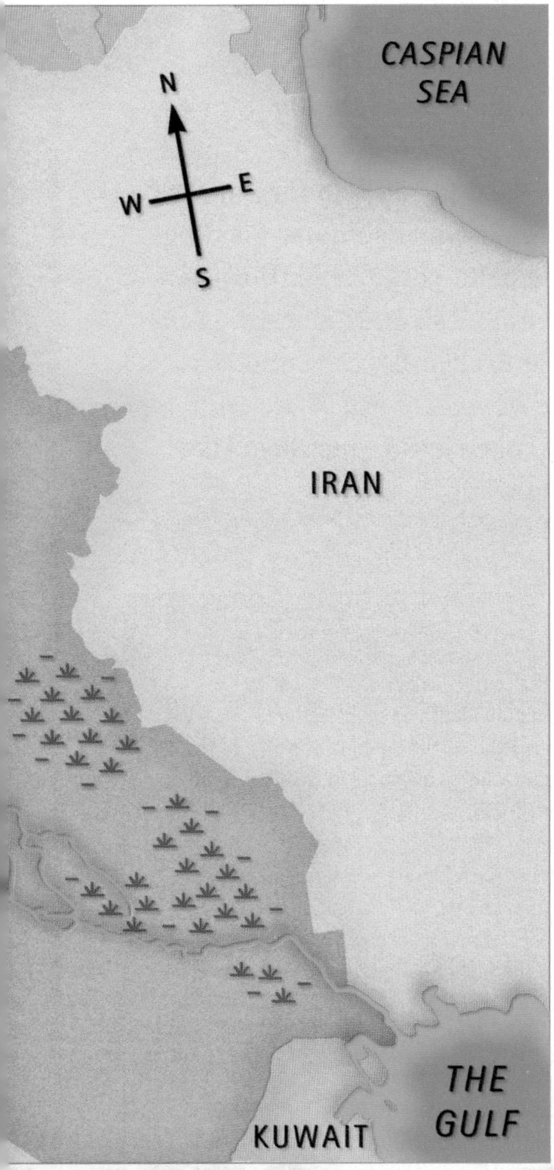

Figure 3: Marsh Arabs, Iraq

Why is it so difficult to manage the use of water in transnational rivers like the Euphrates?

Key Words: algae blooms see page 124

Dam building on the River Nile

▶ Investigation

The River Nile is the world's longest river and has three main branches: the White and Blue Nile and the Atbara [Figure 2]. Each contributes in a different way to the flow of the main river and the work it does.

Discharge is the amount (volume) of water in a river. 30 per cent of the Nile's **discharge** and 3 per cent of its load comes from the White Nile, which starts in Lake Victoria.

The greatest discharge and load comes from the Blue Nile, which begins in the Ethiopian Highlands. Red sediment from the Atbara and Blue Nile used to settle in the Nile Delta during the Nile's annual summer flooding. This made the delta very fertile. However, the opening of the Aswan High Dam in the early 1960s controlled flooding and reduced the sediments deposited [Figure 1]. Sediments now settle in Lake Nasser, the huge lake behind the dam.

▼ Figure 1: The effects of the Aswan High Dam

Advantages	Disadvantages
Power supply: Water from Lake Nasser is used to produce hydro electric power (HEP). This supplies 64% of Egypt's electricity, the equivalent of 2 million tonnes of oil.	**Water loss:** 30% of water that enters Lake Nasser is lost by evaporation and through the ground. Ethiopia has suffered recurring droughts since 1981. This has reduced the amount of water carried by the Blue Nile and Atbara. Less water is available in Lake Nasser to produce hydro electric power (HEP).
Flooding: Summer floods now have much less impact than in the past.	
Food production: 400 000 ha of desert land can now be used to grow crops, using water from new irrigation schemes. This has doubled the amount of arable land in Egypt from 4% to 8%. Irrigation is available all year. This allows three crops to be grown annually. Cash crops such as sugar cane, cotton and maize have increased.	**Fishing industry:** Silt is now trapped behind the dam, so fewer nutrients reach the Mediterranean Sea, badly affecting off-shore fishing for sardine, shrimp, lobster and mackerel. This has cost 30 000 jobs, millions of pounds and the loss of an important food source.
	Salinity: As the water table has risen, it has led to a build up of salt in the soil (salinisation). Over 30% of Egypt's arable land is now at risk.
Transport: Freight (cargo) and cruise ships now navigate the river all year round.	**Brick industry:** Silt from the Nile was used to make bricks. Now brick-makers have to buy expensive topsoil from farmers. This is in short supply, and many farmers are unwilling to sell when they can use it themselves.
Fishing: A new fishing industry catching carp, bass and catfish has developed on Lake Nasser.	**Erosion:** Erosion has increased downstream of the dam. At the Nile Delta some parts are retreating at rates of up to 40 metres per year.
	Earthquakes: In 1981 the dam was affected by a medium-sized earthquake, triggered by the weight of the water on the bedrock.
	Disease: There have been increases in cases of bilharzia and malaria around the dam and the network of irrigation canals.

▼ Figure 2: The River Nile and the Aswan Dam

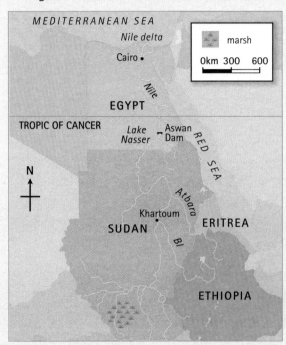

Use the data in **Figure 3** to draw a graph showing the average monthly discharges for the White Nile, Blue Nile and the Atbara.

▼ Figure 3: Average monthly discharges in the Nile Basin (cubic metres per second)

	White Nile	Blue Nile	Atbara
January	829	282	8
February	634	188	2
March	553	156	0
April	525	138	0
May	574	182	1
June	742	461	35
July	897	2080	640
August	1030	5950	2100
September	1130	5650	1420
October	1200	3040	340
November	1200	1030	79
December	1100	499	25
average (annual)	**868**	**1638**	**388**

Study your graph:

- Describe how the seasonal discharge of the White Nile differs from that of the Blue Nile and the Atbara.
- Give reasons for the differences.
- Now look at **Figure 4** and plot the data for silt concentration before and after the building of the Aswan High Dam.

▼ Figure 4 : Silt concentrations in the Nile at Gaafra, before and after the High Dam was built (parts per million)

	Before the dam	After the dam
January	64	44
February	50	47
March	45	45
April	42	50
May	43	51
June	85	49
July	674	48
August	270	45
September	242	41
October	925	43
November	124	48
December	77	47

- Describe the changes in silt concentrations before and after the dam was built.
- What reasons can you think of for these changes?

You have now gathered and analysed information and data on the Nile, its tributaries and the effects of the Aswan High Dam.

- Use what you have learned to design a poster showing:
  - why a dam was needed on the Nile
  - positive and negative impacts of the dam.

You may need to do some additional research before starting your poster, e.g. via an internet search.

6·1 Different types of weather

Look at the photos in **Figure 1** showing different types of weather. What is the weather like in each one?

▲ Figure 1: The UK weather varies from day to day

Weather is the name we give to the state of the **atmosphere**. Weather is happening in the air around us all the time. The type of weather depends on the condition of the air. Air can be hot or cold, wet or dry, heavy or light, still or moving. Usually it is a combination of all of these.

In some locations, like deserts, the weather can be quite similar for days, weeks or months. In other places, like the UK, it can change in just a few hours.

Figure 2 describes the different elements that make up the weather. The most important are **temperature**, **precipitation** and **air pressure**. These affect all the others in the table.

Meteorologists (scientists who study the weather) take thousands of measurements each day using special instruments [**Figure 2**], digital sensors, satellites and observations. These help build up detailed patterns of weather in different locations. They can be used to forecast what type of weather may happen next (pages 102–103).

Think about the ways in which the weather affects your life – what you wear, where you go, what you do, where you go on holiday.

Often the weather can be a nuisance, making us wet when it rains suddenly or stopping us playing sport or having a barbecue. However, for some people weather can affect their jobs and livelihoods or even be a matter of life or death (pages 98–101).

> Make a list of the sort of jobs which can be affected by the weather.

▼ Figure 2: Different types of weather

Weather	Description	Instrument used	Units
Temperature	how hot or cold it is	thermometer	degrees Celsius
Precipitation	moisture falling from the clouds – rain, hail, sleet or snow	rain gauge	
Air pressure	the weight of the air: from heavy to light	barometer or barograph	millibars
Humidity	the amount of moisture in the air: how 'sticky' it feels	hygrometer	percentage
Wind	speed: how fast the air is moving	anemometer	kilometres per hour / knots
	direction: the direction from which the wind is blowing	wind vane	compass direction
Clouds	the amount (and type) of clouds covering the sky	observation	oktas (eighths of the sky)
Visibility	how far you can see: from clear to nothing!	observation	metres
Sunshine	how long the sun shines during each day	sunshine recorder	hours

New Words: atmosphere, temperature, precipitation, air pressure see page 124

6·2 Rain

Page 60 looked at the hydrological or water cycle. One of the main inputs into the cycle – and one of the main elements of the weather – is precipitation. Although this includes rain, hail, sleet and snow, most precipitation falls from clouds as rain.

▼ Figure 1: How rain is formed

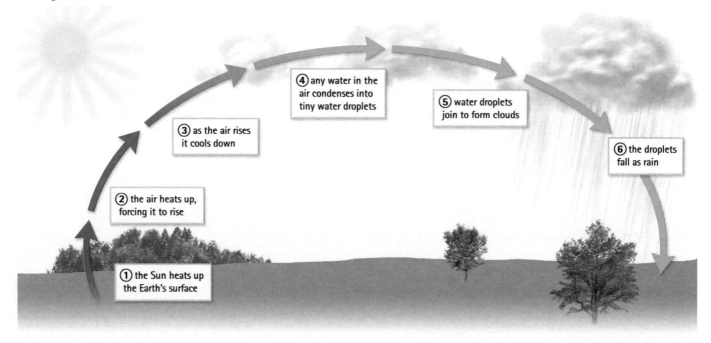

① the Sun heats up the Earth's surface

② the air heats up, forcing it to rise

③ as the air rises it cools down

④ any water in the air condenses into tiny water droplets

⑤ water droplets join to form clouds

⑥ the droplets fall as rain

There are three main types of rainfall – **relief**, **convectional** and **frontal**. The main process by which they are formed is shown in **Figure 1**. However, the reason why the air becomes warm and/or rises is different for each type of rainfall:

- **relief rainfall: prevailing winds** blow warm air towards highland areas forcing it upwards [Figure 3]

- **convectional rainfall:** high temperatures heat the ground, so the resulting warm air rises vertically [Figure 5]

- **frontal rainfall:** a mass of warm air meets a mass of cold air. The air masses cannot mix so the warm air is forced up above the colder, heavier air [Figure 6].

Why is precipitation such an important part of the hydrological cycle?

▼ Figure 2: How clouds form

Clouds contain thousands of tiny floating water droplets which eventually fall as rain

▼ Figure 3: Relief rainfall

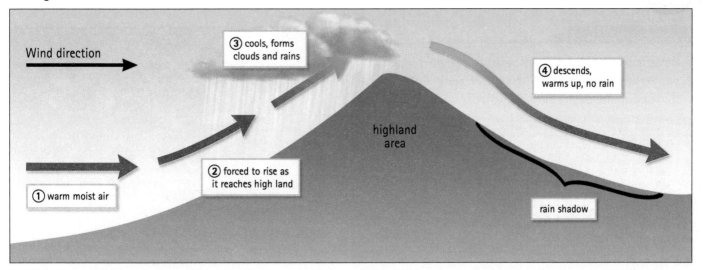

Wind direction

③ cools, forms clouds and rains

④ descends, warms up, no rain

highland area

② forced to rise as it reaches high land

① warm moist air

rain shadow

▼ Figure 4: Relief rainfall over the UK

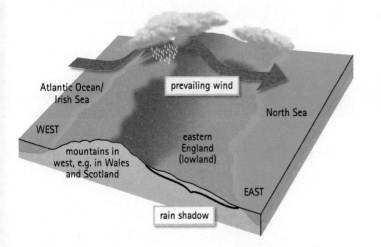

Atlantic Ocean/ Irish Sea

prevailing wind

North Sea

WEST

mountains in west, e.g. in Wales and Scotland

eastern England (lowland)

EAST

rain shadow

▼ Figure 5: Convectional rainfall

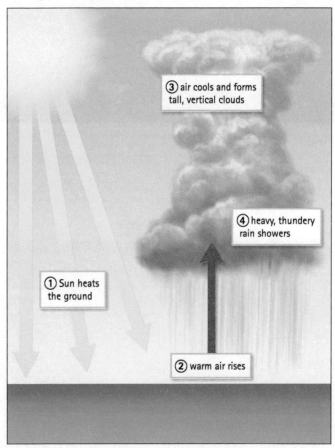

③ air cools and forms tall, vertical clouds

④ heavy, thundery rain showers

① Sun heats the ground

② warm air rises

▼ Figure 6: Frontal rainfall

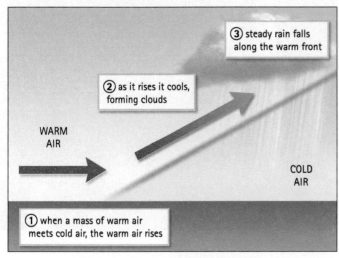

③ steady rain falls along the warm front

② as it rises it cools, forming clouds

WARM AIR

COLD AIR

① when a mass of warm air meets cold air, the warm air rises

Which type of rainfall is the least common in the UK? Why?

Extreme weather

Describe the type of extreme weather shown in each photograph of **Figure 1**. Where in the world do you think each one might have happened?

▲ Figure 1: Examples of extreme weather

Figure 1 shows a range of extreme weather events from around the world. We rarely experience very extreme weather conditions in the UK, although flooding after spells of heavy rain has been more frequent in recent years.

However, in many countries, especially the less wealthy, developing ones (LEDCs), extreme weather is more common. This is when the weather itself becomes a **hazard**. It can create dangerous, life-threatening conditions and cause widespread damage to buildings and the natural environment.

Weather hazards include:
- hurricanes
- tornadoes
- drought
- flooding
- landslides and mudslides.

Some weather hazards, like tornadoes and landslides, often affect quite small areas. Others, like hurricanes and drought, can affect much larger areas. When extreme weather happens, the way people cope with it often depends on whether people live in wealthy MEDCs or poorer LEDCs – and how much warning there is.

The damage done can last for many years, especially in LEDCs where there is little money available to rebuild and recover.

▼ Figure 2: Flooding caused by Hurricane Mitch in Honduras

Hurricanes bring high winds and torrential rain, turning rivers into raging torrents and causing widespread flooding

▼ Figure 3: A survivor's story

'The rain had battered against the house all day – horizontal rods hammering down from a fearsome black sky. I had done everything I could to secure the building as the winds increased in speed and ferocity. As I lay in bed in the darkness, the noise was deafening. The tin roof rattled and shook, preparing to be ripped off as the wind tore into it. The noise from the rain beating down sounded as though someone had turned on a high-pressure hose. The wind was driving some of the rain through the space between the walls and the roof, turning the once hard-baked earth floor into mud. Gradually everything was becoming damp. Above the noise I could still hear trees outside creaking and groaning. The nearby stream was rushing like a torrent, sounding like a high-speed train was about to run through the house. Hurricane Mitch had well and truly arrived in Honduras.'

Have *you* ever experienced extreme weather? Where? What was it like? How did you feel?

6·4 Weather hazards: hurricanes

Hurricanes, also called tropical cyclones or typhoons, are one of the world's most dramatic and destructive weather hazards. Hurricanes are found in the North Atlantic, typhoons in Southeast Asia, and tropical cyclones in South Asia and Africa. They all begin life as areas of very low pressure around the Equator.

If the water is warm enough, tropical storms can develop. **Figure 1** shows how this causes warm air to rise and rotate.

Once wind speeds reach 120 kph, the storm becomes a hurricane.

Most hurricanes last for about ten days. During that time high winds and torrential rain can cause widespread damage, death and injury.

▼ Figure 1: Inside a hurricane

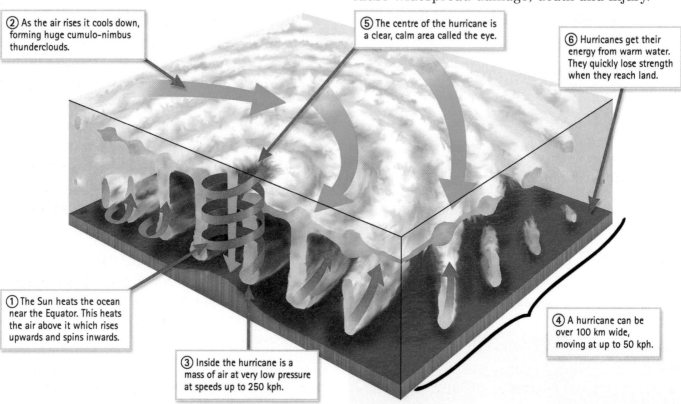

② As the air rises it cools down, forming huge cumulo-nimbus thunderclouds.

⑤ The centre of the hurricane is a clear, calm area called the eye.

⑥ Hurricanes get their energy from warm water. They quickly lose strength when they reach land.

① The Sun heats the ocean near the Equator. This heats the air above it which rises upwards and spins inwards.

④ A hurricane can be over 100 km wide, moving at up to 50 kph.

③ Inside the hurricane is a mass of air at very low pressure at speeds up to 250 kph.

▼ Figure 2: Satellite images of Hurricane Mitch

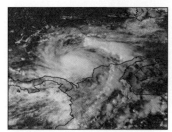

21 October: Mitch reaches hurricane force off South America

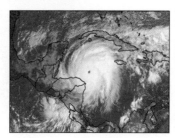

26 October: Now a category 5 hurricane (the highest) with wind speeds of 250 kph

27 October: The eye of the storm is just off Honduras, but even satellite photos could not indicate where it would go next

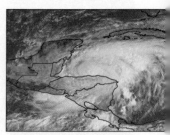

28 October: Although wind speeds started to drop, Mitch was moving very slowly over Honduras and Central America

Key Words: **hurricanes** see page 124

Figure 3: The aftermath of Hurricane Mitch

Mudslides caused many deaths – burying houses, possessions and people

The word hurricane comes from 'Hurican', the Carib God of Evil, and from the Mayan god 'Hurakan' who blew his breath across water.

One of the most destructive hurricanes of recent years was Hurricane Mitch [**Figure 3**]. Mitch hit the Caribbean, Central America and the USA for a ten-day period at the end of October and beginning of November 1998. It killed 20 000 people, made over 3 million homeless, and caused damage estimated at £7 billion.

The worst hit countries were Honduras and Nicaragua, both fairly poor LEDCs that depend heavily on farming. Rain, winds and mudslides destroyed buildings, power and transport links, crops, livestock and farmland.

With little of their own resources to undertake rebuilding, countries like Honduras have had to rely on overseas aid. Money and help has come from organisations like the World Bank, Central America Emergency Trust Fund and charities. However, it is likely to take twenty years or more for the areas hit by Mitch to be rebuilt and for economies to recover.

29 October: Sitting over Central America for three days, Mitch dropped over 180 cm of rain

2 November: Mitch starts to move NE across the Gulf of Mexico

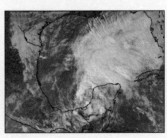

3 November: Mitch reaches Florida and starts to die down

Major hurricanes often hit Florida and neighbouring states in the USA. However, these areas usually recover much more quickly than countries like Honduras. Why?

6·5 Technology and weather forecasting

Thousands of measurements and weather recordings are made every day throughout the UK and sent to the Meteorological or 'Met' Office in Exeter. The Met Office continually collects, processes and maps all this data [Figure 1].

Not only does this provide accurate records of our weather, it can be used to identify patterns and processes. These help meteorologists to predict or forecast future weather and produce maps and charts [Figure 2].

UK weather data is collected by the Met Office from a wide range of locations on land and sea including:

- thirty main weather stations staffed by full-time meteorologists making hourly observations
- observations from local weather stations, for example from coastguards

▼ Figure 1: The Met Office

▼ Figure 2: A weather map, as used by forecasters

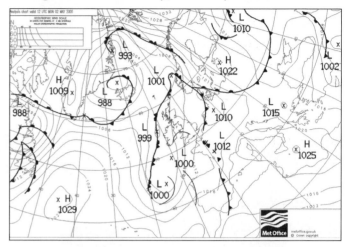

- over fifty automated weather stations
- ships, oil rigs, stationary and moving buoys
- weather balloons (radiosondes).

You can receive weather forecasts for your local area for the next six hours via a text messaging service to your mobile phone. How might this be useful to you and your family?

Many of these methods have been used for hundreds of years, but meteorologists have always been quick to use new technology.

Radar is used to show where and how hard it is raining. It has been used for many years on weather charts to show rain moving across the country.

Today new technology, especially computers and satellites [Figure 3] has revolutionised the way weather is recorded, analysed and forecast.

▼ Figure 3: A weather satellite

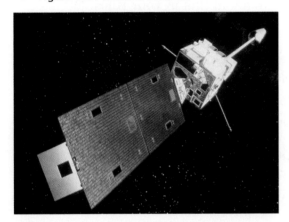

Two types of satellites are used to observe and record weather patterns from space – those which **orbit** the Earth and those which stay in one place. Satellites orbit the Earth from pole to pole in just over an hour and forty minutes. As they do so, the Earth is rotating, so each orbit records different parts of the atmosphere above the Earth [Figure 4]. They give information about temperature and clouds.

With all this data and technology, why aren't weather forecasts always accurate?

Geostationary satellites remain in one place (moving at the same speed as the Earth), usually 36 000 km above the Equator. It takes twenty-four hours for a satellite to orbit the Equator, recording the same area. Their images of clouds help meteorologists to work out wind speed and direction and identify weather systems like tropical cyclones or hurricanes (see pages 100–101).

Advanced computer systems process the vast amount of data that is being continuously collected. They analyse existing data and use complex models and simulations to predict and forecast future weather. This is more than merely useful – in the case of hurricanes it can save lives. This data also helps farmers and water companies in their work.

▼ Figure 4: A weather satellite image

▶ **Investigation**

Task

- To plan, design and make a quiz or simple game based on the information about the weather in Chapter 6.
- To write a series of questions (and answers) to use in your quiz or game to test weather knowledge.
- To decide a simple set of rules for those who take part in the quiz or game.
- To test your game and alter it if necessary.

Note: this task needs to undertaken in small groups or pairs.

What to do

Decide whether you are going to design a quiz or a simple board game. For either, you must draw up a set of questions – at least 100 but probably more. **Do this first**.

In what style or format will your questions be written? For most games or quizzes these are usually on individual cards. If the cards also have the answers, they need to be read out by someone other than the person answering it. If the player needs to look at the card, the answer must be hidden (e.g. on the back of the card so they don't see it). Think about this in your rules.

Are your questions going to be at the same level, or will you have easy and difficult ones? Do players have a choice? Do questions progress from easy to difficult – or is it random? Think about this in your rules.

What type of questions and answers will you have? There are examples on this page to help you decide.

Are all your questions going to be text? Or might some be diagrams, photos or symbols?

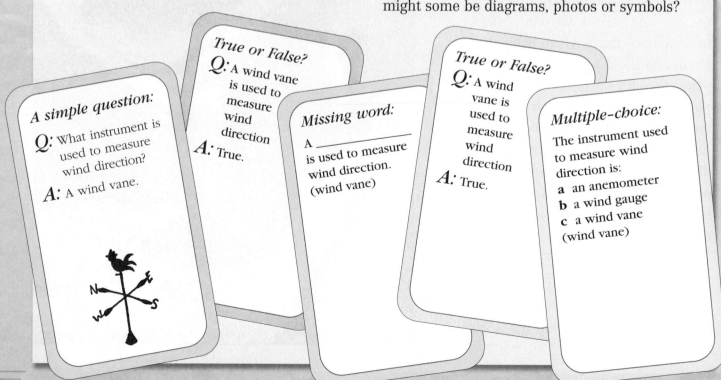

A simple question:

Q: What instrument is used to measure wind direction?

A: A wind vane.

True or False?

Q: A wind vane is used to measure wind direction

A: True.

Missing word:

A _____ is used to measure wind direction. (wind vane)

True or False?

Q: A wind vane is used to measure wind direction

A: True.

Multiple-choice:

The instrument used to measure wind direction is:
a an anemometer
b a wind gauge
c a wind vane
(wind vane)

You may decide to have a mixture of different styles of questions.

Once you have written your cards, you need to decide how they are going to be used and how a player wins.

Quizzes

Think about different quizzes. Examples from television include *The Weakest Link* and *Who Wants to be a Millionaire?* Will your quiz be based on something similar?

Board games

If you are making a board game, keep it simple – you will have to make the board (and pieces) as well as making up the rules

and questions. Some board games have numbered squares. Trivial Pursuit and Monopoly are also board games. How will players move around the board, for example will you need dice?

Rules

A clear set of rules is essential – but don't make them too complicated. Study the rules for existing quizzes and games before your write yours. Are there time limits? Can players be in teams or do they play as individuals? How do they win?

When you have written your rules, test them yourself to see if they work. Then let other people play them.

7·1 What is development?

▼ Figure 1: Each of these images shows a different level of development in different parts of the world

Make a list of the words or phrases that describe what you can see in each photograph in **Figure 1**. Add words that describe what you feel about each one.

Development is an important term used by geographers. It is often used to describe how rich or poor a country or region is. Richer, wealthier countries are called **More Economically Developed Countries** or **MEDCs**. Poorer, less wealthy countries are called **Less Economically Developed Countries** or **LEDCs**. **Figure 2** shows that most MEDCs are found in the Northern Hemisphere, while most LEDCs are in the Southern Hemisphere.

> Can you think of any reasons for the North-South divide in levels of development?

Development also means much more than just how rich or poor a place is. Development is really a process about making improvements in the way people live.

There are many different ways for a region or country to improve the quality of life of its **citizens**. Development can mean different things to different people.

Most people want to make their lives better or easier, but there is often disagreement or conflict between people about how this can be achieved. What are your ideas about development? How would you like your area or country to change and improve?

Your ideas about what you want for the future are tied with where you are living now. This is called being **situated**. A person living in a rural area in a LEDC might have very different views about development from someone living in a MEDC. This is because they are situated differently.

▼ Figure 2: The North-South development divide

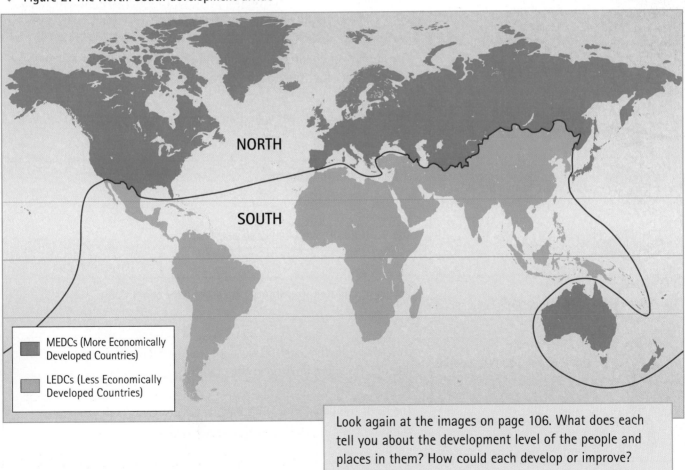

NORTH

SOUTH

■ MEDCs (More Economically Developed Countries)

□ LEDCs (Less Economically Developed Countries)

> Look again at the images on page 106. What does each tell you about the development level of the people and places in them? How could each develop or improve?

Key Words: MEDCs, LEDCs, situated see page 124

7·2 Measuring development

On pages 106–107 we saw that development can mean different things to different people – but how can we accurately decide how developed somewhere is? Look back at the photos you studied on page 106. Rank them in order, most developed first and least developed last.

> How did you decide upon the order of the images? What influenced your choice?

To compare different levels of development, geographers look at **development indicators**. These are sets of data or measurements that can be used to compare countries or places. Figure 1 lists some of the most commonly used ones and what they measure. Since 1990, the United Nations has collected this data and published it every year in their *Annual Human Development Report*. This report now contains hundreds of different development indicators.

▼ Figure 1: Development indicators

Development indicator	Description
Gross Domestic Product (GDP) per capita	A measurement of relative wealth: by taking the money made by a country in a year and dividing it by the population. Measured in $US.
life expectancy	How long you can expect to live, starting from the year you are born. Females usually have a higher life expectancy than males.
infant mortality	The number of children who die before their fifth birthday. Measured per thousand of the population.
growth rate	Births minus deaths per year. Can be a negative figure.
average calories per day	Available diet/food supply.
adult literacy	The % of adults who can read and write.
% in education	The % of children in primary and secondary education.
doctors per 100 000 people	How many doctors per 100 000 people. The higher the number of doctors, the more developed the country.
access to fresh water	The % of the population who have access to clean, safe drinking water.

Key Words: development indicators see page 124

▼ Figure 2: This world map shows GDP

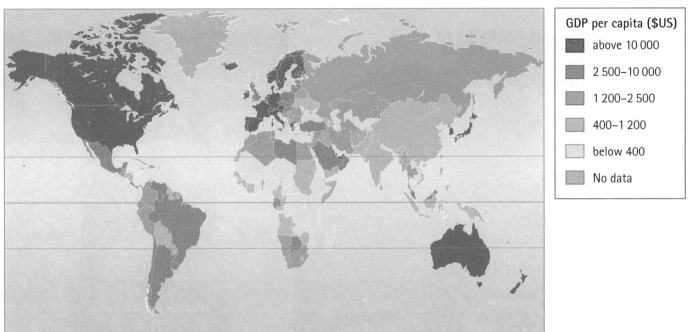

GDP per capita ($US)

- above 10 000
- 2 500–10 000
- 1 200–2 500
- 400–1 200
- below 400
- No data

The different indicators can be divided into a number of groups. The main ones are **economic**, **social** and **environmental**. Traditionally, economic indicators, especially **Gross Domestic Product (GDP)**, have been used to assess levels of development [Figure 2].

GDP is a way of measuring the wealth of a country. It is calculated by taking all the money made by a country in one year, and dividing this by the total population. This gives an average figure of the GDP **per capita** [Figure 2].

> What does **Figure 2** tell you about where the richest countries are?
>
> Is there a pattern? What doesn't it tell you about development?

In theory, the higher the GDP, the richer the country is. However this can be misleading. For example, Kuwait has quite a high GDP, but that does not mean that everyone in Kuwait is wealthy. The majority of the wealth, mainly from selling oil, is owned by a small minority of the population. Most Kuwaitis are much poorer than the figure for GDP would suggest. It is also important to know how this money is spent, for example on building hospitals or buying weapons.

Today, to get a more accurate view of how developed a country or region is, geographers use a range of different indicators together. Health, education, employment, nutrition and clean water are all important factors in development. There are also factors which cannot be measured easily, but they can affect the quality of life – and the development – of a country.

> What don't development indicators tell you about a country? What other factors need to be considered when measuring how 'developed' a country is?

Figure 1: Different aspects of the same place

Unlike the images on page 106, all the photographs here are taken in the USA. Not only are they all from the USA, they are all from one American state: California.

People who live in California complain that when outsiders think of California they only ever imagine San Francisco, Los Angeles or Hollywood. Of course, these places are famous across the world, but there is much more to California than just these.

The photos here show a variety of locations in California, and different levels of development. They demonstrate that development doesn't just vary between countries, but also within countries and even within local areas.

Think about your local area or region: does it contain places with different levels of development? They may not be as contrasting as the images of California shown here, but most places have a range of levels of development.

On pages 108–109 you saw how different development indicators can be used to decide how developed a country is. Look at those indicators again. Could they be used to identify differences *within* a place? What other information would be useful?

▶ Investigation

Asking questions

Many different types of people live in California – in many different places:
- choose one of the photos
- describe who you think might live there and what you imagine they might think of the place
- make a list of seven questions you might want to ask them
- with a partner, discuss what you think their answers to your questions might be
- using your own seven questions, answer them for where *you* live.

7·4 A long life?

Figure 1: Life expectancy across the world

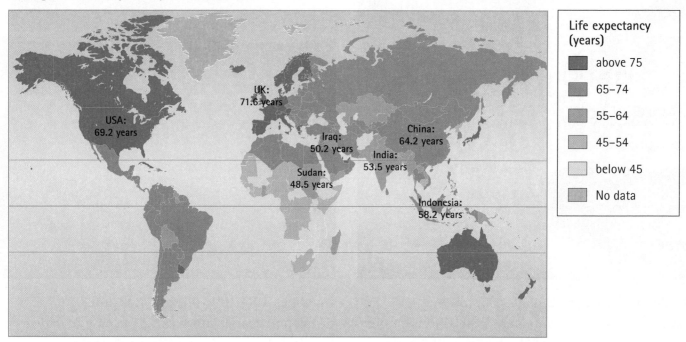

Life expectancy (years)

- above 75
- 65–74
- 55–64
- 45–54
- below 45
- No data

UK: 71.6 years

USA: 69.2 years

Iraq: 50.2 years

China: 64.2 years

India: 53.5 years

Sudan: 48.5 years

Indonesia: 58.2 years

Not everyone across the world enjoys the same level of health. Factors that influence health in a country or region can vary widely. One of the ways that we can judge how healthy people are is to look at the indicator for **life expectancy**. This is the average age that the population of a country can expect to live to (shown on the world map in **Figure 1**).

Look at the life expectancy figures for each of the countries named on the map. They have quite different levels of life expectancy. Some of the reasons for these differences are:

- access to clean water
- access to a good, varied diet
- money to spend on basic health care facilities, for example doctors and hospitals
- living in a peaceful area away from war zones.

Rank the named countries [**Figure 1**] in order of life expectancy – highest first. Try to explain the life expectancy figure for each country.

Good or bad health – and life expectancy – doesn't only depend on the causes of illness and disease. When people get sick, their access to help and treatment can also influence their life expectancy. In the UK, people usually visit their doctor if they are unwell.

Wherever you live in the world, health care has to be paid for. Different countries have different ways of making sure this is done. One way is for the patient to pay the doctor directly. Other ways include people taking out their own health insurance, or paying for health care through their taxes. In extremely poor places, or in emergencies, health care may be provided for free by charity organisations.

Key Words: life expectancy see page 124

▼ Figure 2: Primary health care in India

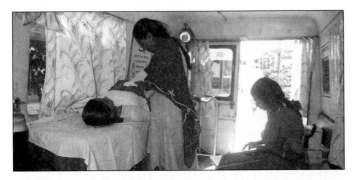

▼ Figure 3: Primary health care in the UK

Where health care is paid for directly by the patients, there are problems when individuals cannot afford to pay. In richer countries these are usually avoided by investment in health insurance and **primary health care**. Primary health care is the first contact you would have with the health system, for example with a local doctor.

Good primary health care does not only provide treatment, it can help prevent serious illness by giving vaccinations and offering health advice.

Secondary health care e.g. hospitals, deals with more serious illness, which is more expensive and difficult to treat. Hospitals are usually found in larger towns and cities, serving large areas. As technological advancements and more medical discoveries are made, the cost of health care increases.

Figure 4 shows a range of indicators related to health in the countries named in **Figure 1**. Some of these help to explain why life expectancy in each country varies. For example, if you study the figures carefully, there is a strong link between life expectancy and the amount of GDP each country spends on health care. Geographers call links between sets of figures **correlations**.

> See if you can find connections or links between other indicators in the table and life expectancy. What other information or indicators would be useful?

▼ Figure 4: Health-related development indicators for seven countries

	China	India	Indonesia	Iraq	Sudan	USA	United Kingdom
Total population (millions)	1 294	1 049	217	24.5	32.9	291	59.1
GDP per capita ($US)	4 580	2 670	3 230	2 997	1 820	35 750	26 150
Life expectancy (years)	70.9	63.7	66.6	61.1	55.5	77.0	78.1
Number of doctors (per 100 000 people)	164	51	16	N/A	16	279	164
Infant mortality (per 1000)	31	67	33	115	64	7	5
Health expenditure per person ($US)	224	80	77	97	39	4 887	1 989

Key Words: primary health care, secondary health care; correlations see page 124

Improving life expectancy

The media often reports global health disasters such as the AIDS epidemic, or drought and famine in countries like the Sudan. However, the overall picture of global health can look more optimistic. **Figure 1** shows how, over time, life expectancy in most countries has improved.

▼ Figure 1: Life expectancy at birth: 1955–2002

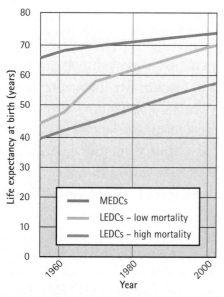

One of the most encouraging developments is that some of the diseases that would have killed us fifty years ago are no longer a threat. For example rickets, a bone-softening disease caused by a vitamin D deficiency, was once common in the UK. The UK government was so concerned that they made milk (a good source of vitamin D) freely available to all children in primary schools. As children started to drink milk regularly at school, rickets became a disease of the past.

In countries where drinking milk is not common, rickets is still a hazard. In the USA, because most young people prefer fizzy drinks to milk, the government has run a 'Got Milk?' campaign [Figure 2] to encourage everyone to drink more milk as part of a healthier diet.

> From what you have already learnt, what are the reasons for these improvements in overall life expectancy?

However, it is clear that most countries with a high life expectancy are MEDCs. Despite global improvements, people in wealthier countries are still living longer than those in LEDCs. This is due to many factors:

- medical advances making some diseases rare
- improved nutrition
- better access to clean water
- improved sanitation
- better health education
- better primary and secondary health care
- a better standard of housing.

▼ Figure 2: Got Milk?

The lifestyle of many people in MEDCs is now leading to other health problems. The **World Health Organisation (WHO)** has warned that people in MEDCs are increasingly suffering from **non-communicable diseases**, for example heart disease, cancer and also stress-related and mental illnesses.

What do we need for good health?

What do we really need to be disease free and healthy? Some needs are universal, such as clean water and good sanitation. What – and how much – we eat is also very important. The UK government now recommends that everyone should eat five portions of fruit and vegetables a day [Figure 3]. We should also limit the amount of fat, sugar and salt we eat. Many processed foods contain high levels of these.

Poor diet is not the only health concern in the UK. Both nicotine and alcohol can seriously damage health and lead to higher risk of cancers and heart disease in later life. Regular exercise (about thirty minutes a day) also helps keep people fit and healthy.

▼ Figure 4: Processed foods and too much alcohol ... a bad combination!

▼ Figure 3: The 'Five-a-day!' campaign

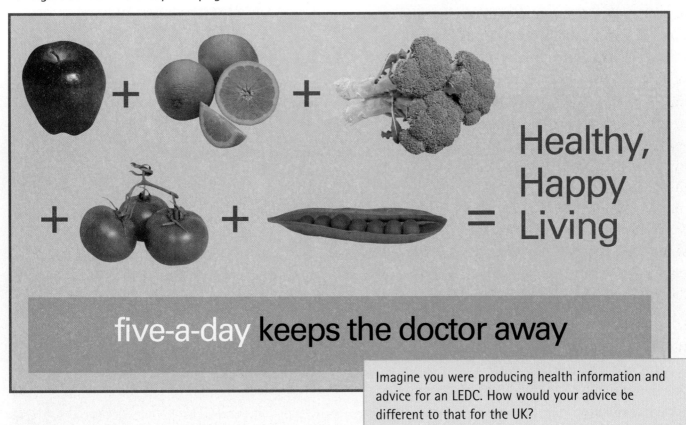

Healthy, Happy Living

five-a-day keeps the doctor away

Imagine you were producing health information and advice for an LEDC. How would your advice be different to that for the UK?

Key Words: World Health Organisation (WHO), non-communicable diseases see page 124

7·6 The geography of disease

Over the past fifty years, the number of people dying from curable diseases has fallen dramatically in some places. New discoveries in medicine have helped to develop treatments for illnesses that would once have proved fatal. However, there are still millions of unnecessary deaths every year, especially among children.

Mapping cholera

For 200 years, doctors tried to find the cause of cholera. It is a dreadful disease which causes diarrhoea, vomiting and even death. In the nineteenth century there was a particularly bad outbreak of cholera in London, and the reasons for this puzzled doctors.

John Snow, a geographer, decided to map the outbreaks of cholera [Figure 1]. Once he had completed his map, it was clear that the centre of each outbreak was a shared water pump. Further investigations proved that cholera is frequently spread by dirty water.

▼ Figure 1: Snow's map of cholera outbreaks

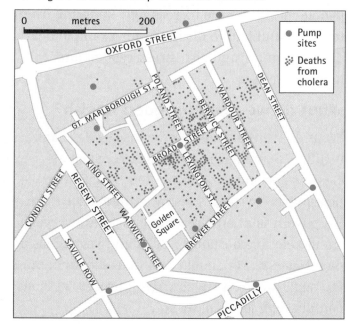

▼ Figure 2: Dirty water in a shanty town (LEDC)
Cholera is easily spread in situations like this where dirty water is found close to houses

Measles

Although measles is a disease that is preventable by **inoculating** toddlers and babies, each year it kills nearly one million children. Half of these deaths are in Africa, making measles the single leading cause of vaccine-preventable deaths among children there.

Unfortunately, the situation is made worse because measles is a **contagious** disease and will spread quickly when people live close together. The measles virus is easily spread in airborne droplets from the coughs and sneezes of infected people. We don't need to map the outbreak of measles to find the cause, because we know how it is spread and how it can be treated. However, finding out where outbreaks occur can help aid agencies to direct money and help to where they are most needed.

Tuberculosis (TB)

Despite the development of a cure for TB more than fifty years ago, the disease still kills 2–3 million people every year. Nearly 98 per cent of all cases are found in LEDCs. However, a worrying trend is that the incidence of TB in countries like the UK is on the increase. By the year 2020, the World Health Organisation (WHO) estimates that 36 million people will die of TB if the disease is not treated. But why?

One theory is that when people live close to each other they are more likely to catch TB – a good reason why high housing density is not a good idea.

▼ **Figure 3: Vaccinating children in a LEDC clinic**
This child is being vaccinated against measles

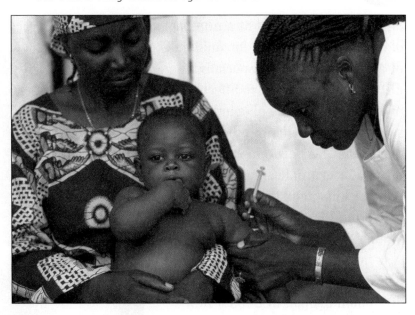

▼ **Figure 4: How TB is spread**

'TB is a disease of the lungs spread through the air from one person to another. When a person with TB coughs or sneezes, bacteria are put into the air. People nearby can breathe in these bacteria and become infected themselves.

When TB bacteria are breathed in, they settle in the lungs. Once there, the bacteria can begin to grow, moving through the blood to other parts of the body, such as the kidney, spine and brain.'

Geographers have also played an important role in mapping where diseases occur, helping to find the causes, and showing where help is most needed. Knowing and understanding where diseases occur is an important part of trying to stop them from spreading.

7·7 SARS – a new global disease

Pages 116–117 looked at a number of diseases responsible for millions of deaths every year, especially in LEDCs. All of them have affected people for hundreds of years. While some diseases remain, others disappear and new ones take their place. For example smallpox, once a major killer, has been virtually wiped out thanks to the availability of an affordable vaccine. The 1970s saw the rise of HIV/AIDS, a virus which has so far killed over 40 million people. In 2003 a new virus, **SARS**, spread across the world with frightening speed.

What is SARS?

As the name suggests, Severe Acute Respiratory Syndrome (SARS) is a virus that affects the lungs. Early symptoms are similar to flu – headache, sore throat, fever and coughing. It is spread mainly by coughing and sneezing. It has a mortality rate of about 4 per cent. In 1993 four people in every hundred infected died.

There is no specific medicine or vaccine for SARS. However doctors successfully treated many of those infected by using a range of

▼ Figure 2: Screening passengers, Changi Airport, Singapore

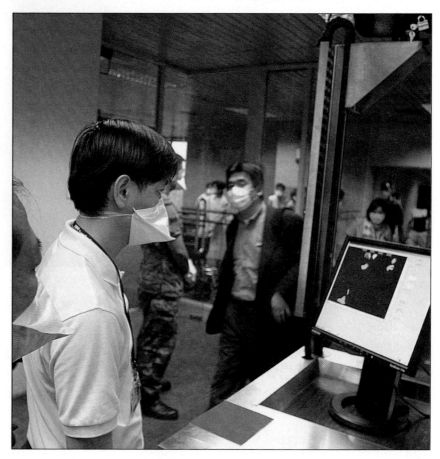

Airport staff use 'Infrared Fever Screening' on passengers arriving from Hong Kong. Ths can identify those with high temperatures who may be carrying the SARS virus.

existing drugs – especially those cases that were diagnosed early.

Figure 3 shows where the SARS outbreak began and how it spread. During this time there were over 10 000 cases and 800 deaths.

▼ Figure 1: The SARS timeline

Nov 2002	Feb 2003	March 2003	End March
First case of SARS in Guangduong, China.	Over 300 people infected and five deaths in Guangduong – the first real recognition of the new virus.	WHO names SARS as a global health threat with suspected cases in Hong Kong, Indonesia, Singapore, the Philippines, Thailand, Vietnam and Canada. New cases in Europe (Spain, Germany, UK and Slovenia).	WHO issues travel warnings; health screening introduced for departing travellers.

Key Words: SARS see page 124

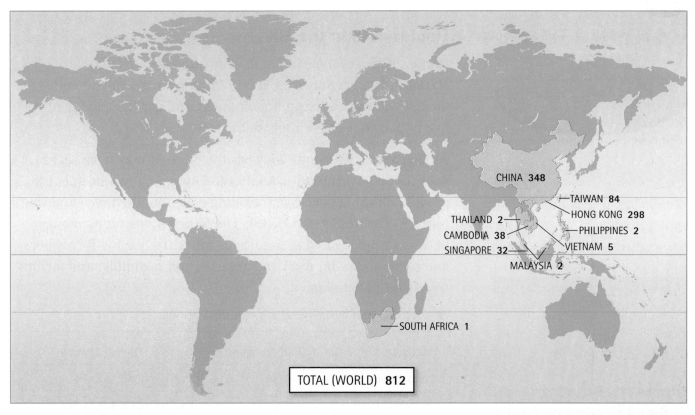

Figure 3: SARS deaths plotted on a world map (2002–2003)

CHINA 348 · TAIWAN 84 · HONG KONG 298 · THAILAND 2 · CAMBODIA 38 · PHILIPPINES 2 · SINGAPORE 32 · VIETNAM 5 · MALAYSIA 2 · SOUTH AFRICA 1

TOTAL (WORLD) 812

The spread of SARS

SARS spread far more quickly – and further – than flu **epidemics** of earlier years. In 1918, the Spanish flu epidemic was spread by people travelling on trains and by troops on ships. It is estimated to have killed 30–40 million people.

Today air travel is affordable and convenient and people can easily fly across the world. This has helped the process of globalisation but also speeded up the worldwide spread of diseases like SARS. It took only days for SARS to travel from China (where it began) to Canada and Europe.

It is quite difficult to diagnose SARS in its early stages because the symptoms are very similar to other illnesses like flu. Isolating those infected and **quarantining** people in contact with them helped restrict the spread of SARS. The World Health Organisation played an important role in recognising SARS as a 'worldwide health threat', issuing warnings about travel.

What made it so difficult to stop SARS spreading? Could other action have been taken to prevent the 812 deaths it caused?

April 2003	May 2003	June 2003	July 2003	January 2004
WHO recommends a ban on non-essential travel to Hong Kong, Guangduong and Canada. Beijing schools and entertainment venues shut for two weeks. Suspected SARS cases in Africa and India. Asian health ministers meet in Malaysia to discuss crisis.	10 000 quarantined in Nanjing, China. Over sixty new cases in one day in Taiwan.	Travel warnings withdrawn. Several countries removed from WHO infected list including China and Hong Kong.	Canada and Taiwan declared SARS free.	Three new cases in China: WHO has evidence that the virus can be carried by **civets**.

Health care

▼ Figure 1: How we pay for the NHS

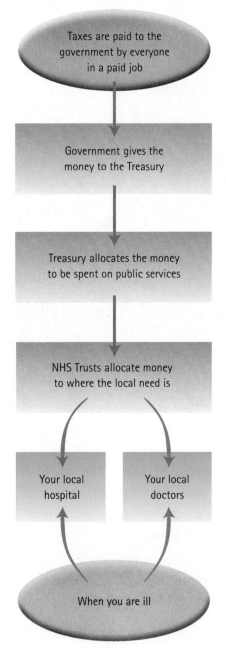

Health care in the UK

In the UK, everyone can get their health care through the **National Health Service (NHS)**. When we need the doctor or dentist, we can make an appointment and get the treatment we need – but that doesn't mean it is free.

All taxpayers contribute towards the NHS. Money from taxes goes to the government who decide how much can be spent to provide different services, including education, defence and the National Health Service (NHS). The NHS divides up its money between primary and secondary health care, paying for doctors and other staff who work in surgeries and hospitals, and for the treatment patients need.

▼ Figure 2: How much operations cost (NHS price list)

Procedure	2008 Estimate	Current Cost
Cataract operation	£786	£763 to £1 164
Heart valve surgery	£10 199	£7 294 to £9 788
Heart bypass	£8 080	£2 540 to £6 911
Hip replacement	£5 568	£4 111 to £5 319
Knee replacement	£6 182	£4 695 to £5 788

In 1998, the UK spent £46 billion on the NHS – an average of £790 per person. This is 7 per cent of the UK's GDP (how much the country earns). The problem is that as technology and medical knowledge improves we can treat more and more diseases – but this costs extra money. The NHS has to decide how many operations it can carry out and which treatments it can afford to provide. Lack of money resources can result in people having to wait for an operation they need.

People already have to pay for **prescriptions** for medicines and a proportion of the costs of dental treatment.

▼ Figure 3: Some key words

Primary health care – the **first** step in health care – this can involve your local doctor, or dentist or optician.

Secondary health care – this is the **second** step in health care, and might involve a trip to a hospital or to see a specialist.

Words: National Health Service (NHS), prescriptions see page 124

Health care in the USA

Not all countries pay for health care as in the UK. In the USA, health care is mostly paid for by private insurance, and is among the most expensive in the world. Individuals can either take out their own insurance or get their insurance paid for by their employers. This pays for most medical costs – but should someone lose their job, or have expenses beyond the limits of their medical insurance, they could be left without any medical care.

It is estimated that 42.6 million people in the USA don't have medical insurance. There is free medical care available but it is of a lower quality and only available to the elderly, those who have been involved in the armed forces, the disabled and the very poor. Becoming ill can involve running up large debts.

How can we judge whether or not a country has a good health care system? What information might you use to help you do this?

▼ Figure 5: Protest rally, New York

An elderly couple taking part in a rally against cuts to the Medicare health scheme in the USA.

▼ Figure 4: A private, well-equipped hospital in the USA

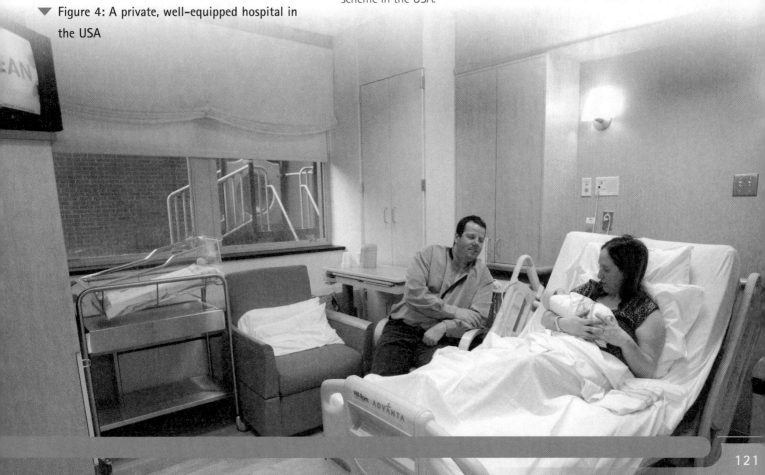

▶ **Investigation**

Spread of a virus

In January 2003, American newspapers predicted a huge outbreak of bird flu. By October 2003, headlines were hitting Russian newspapers with the same fear. But what causes bird flu and how does it travel?

▼ Figure 1: A newspaper extract on 'bird flu'

▼ Figure 2: Areas affected by bird flu

Russian Expert Says Bird Flu Epidemic May Kill Over One Billion This Year

A Russian expert said that US researchers have data suggesting that bird flu could cause up to 700 000 people to fall ill in the USA. The population of the United States is about the same as Russia and the number of cases would also be about the same. He said 'We are half a step away from a worldwide pandemic catastrophe. The death rate among those who contract this type of flu can be as high as 70 per cent'.

The bird flu virus has been discovered in migrant birds living in the Novosibirsk region in Siberia in Russia. Ducks and geese are thought to have brought the virus from Southeast Asia. Although direct contact with migrant birds carrying the virus is unlikely, it could be transmitted to birds who live permanently in Novosibirsk. From there it could be passed on to animals and people. There is a large goose farm near one of the lakes where the migrant birds are found.

A person can become infected by the bird flu through contact with pigs. 'Pigs transmit this disease without obvious symptoms and it can be transmitted without being noticed,' a spokesman said.

▼ Figure 3: Ekaterina's problems

'My name is Ekaterina, and I live in a rural area in northern Russia that you probably know as Siberia. We have heard that there might be a new flu epidemic called bird flu, and I'm worried. The experts tell us that it could kill lots of people and I'm anxious that my family might be at risk. I live with my parents and my old grandmother and I'm afraid that she might be vulnerable to any strong flu. **Should we move to the city? Will it be safer there?**

- Read the information on pages 122-123. Use the cards in figure 4 to help you decide:

  – Should Ekaterina and her family stay in Siberia?

  – Should they move to the city to try and escape from bird flu?

- What other information would you like to help you make up your mind?

- What would you advise Ekaterina's family to do? Why?

▼ Figure 4: Bird flu cards

Bird flu is only dangerous to humans when it is caught alongside human flu.

Bird flu can only be caught by people who are in regular contact with infected birds.

Old people are more vulnerable to catching flu.

Vaccinations are available against normal flu.

There are very few people living in Siberia, and the cities are characterised by high unemployment.

The winter of 2003 saw a huge outbreak of bird flu in Indonesia and surrounding areas in Southeast Asia.

Bird flu is carried by infected birds that migrate from places where the infection is high.

Siberia has extremely cold winters, where the temperature often drops to below minus 50ºC.

The earth in Siberia is frozen most of the time, so growing crops is not really possible. Most farmers have grazing cattle.

Glossary

Air pressure the weight of the air on the Earth's surface

Algae blooms sudden increases in algae in water caused by temperature changes or chemicals

Aquifer rock which holds water e.g. chalk

Arid very dry. Arid areas receive less than 250mm of rain per year

Atmosphere the layer of air between the Earth's surface and space

Bedload the material carried by a river e.g. sand

Brownfield sites land that has already been built on, but is now derelict and may be used again

Central Business District (CBD) the area in the centre of a town that has shops, offices and administrative functions such as a town hall. The land is expensive here and, as a result, buildings are often multi-storey

Commuters people who travel to work each day, sometimes quite long distances

Contagious something, e.g. a disease, which is spread by close contact between people

Contour ploughing ploughing along the line of contour or slope of the land

Conurbation where a city and its surrounding towns have grown and joined together to form one large urban area e.g. Greater London

Correlations using two sets of data to make comparisons

Counter-urbanisation this is also known as rural-urban migration. It is the movement of people from the towns to the countryside

Culverted where a river has been covered over or channelled through pipes

Deforestation large-scale cutting down of trees

Delta where the river at its mouth deposits lots of sediment, splitting it into many smaller channels e.g. Nile

Deposition the process of dumping material by something e.g. sediments by a river or the sea

Depressions low pressure weather systems that produce wind and rain

Desertification the process by which land becomes arid and desert-like, often through overuse

Development indicators data collected to compare how developed a country or place is e.g. GDP

Discharge the amount of water (volume) in a river

Dormitory town a settlement where many of the inhabitants commute to work and so only go home to sleep during the week

Drainage basin the area of land drained by a particular river and its tributaries

Embankments (see levees) raised banks on either side of a river channel

Enclaves an area enclosed by a wall, often with guards, to keep the inhabitants separate from those in the surrounding area

Epidemic when an infectious disease becomes widespread in a particular place at one time

Erosion the wearing away of something e.g. rivers eroding the land

Flash floods a sudden flood that happens quickly e.g. after a storm

Flood plain the land next to a river covered by water when a river bursts its banks (floods)

Flow the movement from one place to another of water

Freight goods carried by a variety of transport methods e.g. rail, road, sea, air

Functions the services offered by a settlement e.g. the administrative services of a capital city

Geographical Information System (GIS) maps that use a wide range of data or information to build up maps made from different layers for specific purposes

Globalisation the move towards having everything at a worldwide scale; for example, due to globalisation a company making cars will have factories and offices in many different countries

Global Positioning System (GPS) a map system which uses satellite signals to accurately locate where something is at any given time e.g. a person travelling in a car

Gradient slope/steepness

Green belt an area surrounding a large city or conurbation that is not to be built upon but is, wherever possible, preserved as open space. Introduced in the UK in 1947 to prevent urban sprawl

Greenfield site a site for development that has not already been built upon. It is often an open space in a rural area

Gross Domestic Product (GDP) a measurement of the wealth of a country

Hierarchy the placing of objects in order of importance e.g. isolated dwelling, hamlet, village, town and city

High order High order goods are high value goods that are bought only occasionally. They are often luxury items, for example, furniture and jewellery. High order shops sell high order goods

Hurricanes also called cyclones or tropical storms. They are a result of low pressure weather systems bringing high winds and torrential rain

Hypothesis a statement to be proved or disproved through scientific research

Impermeable rock which will not allow water to soak into it

Infrastructure the structure around something e.g. services like electricity and transport

Inner city an area of older, often 19th century terraced houses with corner shops found outside the CBD. It has experienced a lot of change and is often known as the 'zone in transition'

Inoculating giving a vaccination to help prevent disease

Inputs things which go into a system e.g. precipitation in the Water Cycle

Irrigation the artificial watering of land

Labour workers

Lateral erosion wearing away of land in a sideways or outward direction

Latitude distance in degrees north and south of the equator, shown by horizontal lines

LEDCs Less Economically Developed Countries – poorer or developing countries

Levees (see embankments) raised banks either side of a river channel

Life expectancy how many years a person can expect to live from birth

Longitude distance in degrees east or west of 0 degrees, shown by vertical lines

Low order Low order goods are low value goods bought on a daily or regular basis. They are often called convenience goods e.g. bread, milk and newspapers

Meander a bend in a river

MEDCs More Economically Developed Countries – richer or developed countries

Megacities large cities with more than 10 million inhabitants

Migrate/migration to move from one place to another e.g. from the countryside to a city or from one country to another

National Health Service (NHS) the system in the UK that provides free health care at the point of service, funded by National Insurance contributions

Natural increase the amount a population grows, calculated by deducting the death rate from the birth rate

New Towns An urban area in the UK centrally planned by the government and set up to take population from the overcrowded cities after World War 2

NIMBYS 'Not In My Back Yard' People who do not like their local area being developed and changed

Nomadic people who do not settle permanently, but move from place to place

Non-communicable diseases illnesses that cannot be transmitted from one person to another e.g. heart disease

Non-renewable resources that cannot easily be replaced or renewed

Outputs things that come out at the end of a system

Ox bow lake a small lake which was once a river meander but has now been cut off from the river

Per capita per head / per person

Philosophies the search for truth and knowledge concerning the universe, human existence, perception and behaviour pursued by means of reflection, reasoning and argument

Potable water water which is clean enough to drink

Precipitation moisture falling from clouds as rain, sleet or snow

Prescriptions a written slip issued and signed by a doctor to allow medicine or drugs to be given

Prevailing winds the main direction from which winds normally blow

Primary health care the initial contact a person has with their doctor

Processes changes caused by human or physical activity e.g. erosion by a river

Projections different views or representations of the Earth's surface e.g. Mercator, Peters'

Pull factor something positive that makes people want to move into an area

Push factor something negative that makes people want to move away from an area

Quarantining isolating people (or animals) who may have been exposed to a contagious disease

Recycle the re-use of resources / materials e.g. paper, glass

River channel the land between the bed and banks containing the river's water

Runoff water which drains or 'runs off' the land's surface

Rural an area of countryside, the opposite of urban

Rural deprivation the lack of services, such as shops and public transport, which can make the quality of life in the countryside poor, particularly for those who do not have private transport

Rural-urban migration the movement of people from the countryside to towns and cities

Sanitation public health and hygiene – often used to describe facilities to remove waste and dirty water

SARS Severe Acute Respiratory Syndrome

Saturated waterlogged or full of water

Secondary health care places that a doctor may refer people to such as hospitals

Sediments particles of rock which have been worn down into small pieces e.g. mud and sand, often transported and deposited by rivers

Semi-arid dry areas which receive between 250–500mm of rain per year

Services the shops and other facilities offered by a settlement; e.g. schools and hospitals

Shanty towns a group of unplanned shelters constructed from cheap or waste materials and with no basic services, commonly located on the outskirts of cities in LEDCs. Also called squatter settlements

Site the land a settlement is built on

Situated where someone or something is located in relation to other factors

Situation the area surrounding a settlement

Sphere of influence the area around a settlement that is affected by it. For example, the area from which people travel to use a settlement's facilities e.g. shops

Squatter settlements see shanty towns

Stores places where things are held in a system e.g. water in a lake

Suburb a residential district located on the edge of a town or city

Sustainable resources/things which can be used over and over again or replaced

System where inputs, stores and outputs work together as a whole e.g. the Water Cycle

Temperature a measurement of how hot or cold somewhere is

Threshold the number of people needed by a business to be able to run at a profit. For example, a village with a population of 800 will not have enough potential customers to allow a McDonalds to be opened, but there should be enough to allow a general store to survive

Tidal the part of a river (nearest the sea) where water levels change between high and low tide

Trans National Companies (TNCs) large companies that operate in many different countries across the world

Transportation the process of moving something from one place to another

United Nations (UN) global organisation formed in 1945 to promote peace, security and cooperation. Works through various committees and organisations e.g. WHO

Unsustainable the use of resources in such a way that they are used up or cannot be replaced

Urban a built up area, the opposite of rural

Urban-rural fringe the area of land immediately around the town. It may be an area of green belt

Urban-rural migration this is also known as counter-urbanisation. It is the movement of people from the towns to the countryside

Urbanisation the process that causes cities to grow and populations to become more urban

Vertical erosion wearing away downwards into the land

Water balance the amount if water left once evaporation and transpiration losses are taken away from precipitation gains. Can be a positive or negative figure

World Bank international organisation which helps provide financial aid to countries

World Health Organisation (WHO) part of the United Nations

Photo Acknowledgments

The Publishers are grateful to the following for their permission to reproduce copyright photographs:

Advertising Archives: p114; **Alamy:** pp8(background) (Coston Stock), 28 (Nicholas Pitt), 34 (Ingram Publishing), 43(b) (Stan Gamester/Photofusion), 57 (Philip Wolmuth), 77(m) (Holt Studios), 85 (Network Photographers), 99 (Popperfoto), 106(tr) (oote boe), 110(br) (Photo Network), 110(tr) (Shotfile), 111(tl) (David L Moore), 123 (Vladimir Godnik); **Bluesky International:** pp40(r), 41(b), **Bridgeman Art Library:** 6(bl) (Victoria & Albert Museum), 10(b) (by Richard of Haldingham & Lafford c.1290 (Vellum) No_data/Hereford Cathedral, Herefordshire, UK), 25 (Anonymous/Kunsthistorisches Museum, Vienna, Austria; **Comstock:** p115 (Food Icons Royalty Free CD); **Corbis:** pp4 (Matthias Kulka), 6(br) (Gianni Dagli Orti), 6(tl) (Bettmann), 21(b) (Sygma/Durand Patrick), 26(background) (First Light), 35(m) (Conde Nast Archive), 35(tl) (Bettmann), 35(tr) (Bettmann), 35(bl) (H Armstrong Roberts), 35(br) (Bettmann), 36(tr) (Howard Davies), 38/39(background) (Ray Juno), 78(t), (Craig Lovell), 87(r) (Howard Davies), 90 (Ed Kashi), 98(tl) (Sygma/Manuel Jen Francois), 98(br) (Yann Arthus-Bertrand), 101(t) (Bisson Bernard), 103(l), 110(tl) (Robert Holmes), 110(bl) (Lynn Goldsmith), 111(tr) (Royalty Free), 121(t) (Viviane Moos), 121(b) (Najlah Feanny); **©Crown Copyright/Dotted Eyes Ltd:** pp40(l), 41(t);**©Crown Copyright/Ordnance Survey. All rights reserved:** 12(l), 12(r), 17, 58, 70, inside back cover; **DK:** pp 20/21, 100(t); **Empics:** p98(tr) (EPA), 106(tl) (EPA); **Mary Evans Picture Library:** 13(b); **Eye Ubiquitous:** p106(br) (Bennett Dean); **Getty Images:** pp 23(tl) (Taxi), 23(bl) (Food Pix), 34 (background) (Hulton Archive), 44(b) (Julian Herbert), 52 (Taxi), 69 (Image Bank), 87(l) (AFP), 113(b) (Taxi), 118 (Luis Enrique); **Ronald Grant Archive:** p33; **Image State:** p103(r) (Douglas Arnold); **Thomas Kruse:** p29; **Mansell plc:** p8 (with thanks to Allenbourne School, Wimbourne, Dorset); **Nigel Marchant:** p44(t); **Meteorological Office, UK:** pp13(m), 102; **NOAA:** pp100/101 (b); **Panos:** pp51 (Mark Henley), 81(t) (Mikkel Ostergaard), 81(b) (Giacomo Pirozzi), 98(bl) (Bruce Paton), 106(bl) (Mark Henley), 113(t) (Peter Barker), 117 (Giacomo Pirozzi); **Rex:** pp5(r), 31, 32(b) (Paramount/Everett), 32(t) (Paramount/Everett), 35(background), 122(background); **Science Photo Library:** 6(tr), 6(tm), 30(t); **Reid Smith:** pp5(l), 23(r); **Thames Water:** p84; **Topfoto:** p35(tm); **Tropix:** p116; **Gerry Walden:** p9; **webbaviation.co.uk:** p67.

The photos on p24 are
© **PhotoDisc**, **Hemera Technologies Inc** and **Ingram Publishing**.

The cover photograph is © **Corbis/Matthias Kulka**.

The following photos have been supplied by the authors: 27(both), 30(b), 36(tl), 36(bl), 36(br), 42(background), 43(tl), 43(tr), 43(mt), 43(mb), 45(background), 47(l), 47(r), 48(l), 48(r), 49(all), 54, 55(all,) 56(both), 58/59(background), 65(tl), 73(both), 74, 75(both), 76, 77(b), 79(both), 80, 82, 83(both), 86, 88(both), 89, 92/93(background), 94(all), 95(background), 96.

Picture Research by: Hilary Luckcock.

Every effort has been made to trace the copyright holders and we apologise in advance for any unintentional omissions. We would be pleased to insert the appropriate acknowledgement in any subsequent edition of this publication.

Pearson Education Limited

Edinburgh Gate
Harlow
Essex CM20 2JE
England

© Pearson Education Limited 2005

The right of Olly Phillipson, Clare Brooks, Karen Holdich and Garrett Nagle to be identified as the authors of this Work has been asserted by them in accordance with the Copyright, Designs and Patents Acts, 1988.

First published 2005

ISBN 1405800380

Illustrations by Mark Duffin, Willie Ryan and Reid Smith

Picture research by Hilary Luckcock